5558 8213

OPPOSING
VIEWPOINTS®
SERIES

Behavioral Disorders

Other Books of Related Interest:

Opposing Viewpoints Series

Alternative Medicine

Eating Disorders

Health Care

At Issue Series

Alcohol Abuse

Can Diets Be Harmful?

How Does Advertising Impact Teen Behavior?

Current Controversies Series

Alternative Therapies

Vaccines

Anger Management

"Congress shall make
no law . . . abridging
the freedom of speech,
or of the press."

First Amendment to the US Constitution

The basic foundation of our democracy is the First Amendment guarantee of freedom of expression. The Opposing Viewpoints Series is dedicated to the concept of this basic freedom and the idea that it is more important to practice it than to enshrine it.

OPPOSING
VIEWPOINTS®
SERIES

Behavioral Disorders

Roman Espejo, Book Editor

GREENHAVEN PRESS
A part of Gale, Cengage Learning

GALE
CENGAGE Learning·

Detroit • New York • San Francisco • New Haven, Conn • Waterville, Maine • London

Elizabeth Des Chenes, *Director, Content Strategy*
Cynthia Sanner, *Publisher*
Douglas Dentino, *Manager, New Product*

WCN: 01-100-101

For more information, contact:
Greenhaven Press
27500 Drake Rd.
Farmington Hills, MI 48331-3535
Or you can visit our Internet site at gale.cengage.com

For product information and technology assistance, contact us at

Gale Customer Support, 1-800-877-4253
For permission to use material from this text or product, submit all requests online at www.cengage.com/permissions

Further permissions questions can be emailed to permissionrequest@cengage.com

Articles in Greenhaven Press anthologies are often edited for length to meet page requirements. In addition, original titles of these works are changed to clearly present the main thesis and to explicitly indicate the author's opinion. Every effort is made to ensure that Greenhaven Press accurately reflects the original intent of the authors. Every effort has been made to trace the owners of copyrighted material.

Cover image copyright © BSIP SA/Alamy.

LIBRARY OF CONGRESS CATALOGING-IN-PUBLICATION DATA

Behavioral disorders / Roman Espejo, book editor.
    pages cm. -- (Opposing viewpoints)
    Includes bibliographical references and index.
    ISBN 978-0-7377-6949-4 (hardback) -- ISBN 978-0-7377-6950-0 (paperback)
    1. Behavior disorders in children. 2. Behavior disorders in children--Juvenile literature. 3. Problem children--Behavior modification--Juvenile literature. I. Espejo, Roman, 1977- editor of compilation.
    RJ506.B44B435 2014
    618.92'89--dc23
                                                            2013037192

Printed in the United States of America
    1 2 3 4 5   18 17 16 15 14

Contents

Chapter 4: What Policies Will Best Address the Challenges of Behavioral Disorders?

Why Consider Opposing Viewpoints?

"The only way in which a human being can make some approach to knowing the whole of a subject is by hearing what can be said about it by persons of every variety of opinion and studying all modes in which it can be looked at by every character of mind. No wise man ever acquired his wisdom in any mode but this."

John Stuart Mill

In our media-intensive culture it is not difficult to find differing opinions. Thousands of newspapers and magazines and dozens of radio and television talk shows resound with differing points of view. The difficulty lies in deciding which opinion to agree with and which "experts" seem the most credible. The more inundated we become with differing opinions and claims, the more essential it is to hone critical reading and thinking skills to evaluate these ideas. Opposing Viewpoints books address this problem directly by presenting stimulating debates that can be used to enhance and teach these skills. The varied opinions contained in each book examine many different aspects of a single issue. While examining these conveniently edited opposing views, readers can develop critical thinking skills such as the ability to compare and contrast authors' credibility, facts, argumentation styles, use of persuasive techniques, and other stylistic tools. In short, the Opposing Viewpoints Series is an ideal way to attain the higher-level thinking and reading skills so essential in a culture of diverse and contradictory opinions.

In addition to providing a tool for critical thinking, Opposing Viewpoints books challenge readers to question their own strongly held opinions and assumptions. Most people form their opinions on the basis of upbringing, peer pressure, and personal, cultural, or professional bias. By reading carefully balanced opposing views, readers must directly confront new ideas as well as the opinions of those with whom they disagree. This is not to simplistically argue that everyone who reads opposing views will—or should—change his or her opinion. Instead, the series enhances readers' understanding of their own views by encouraging confrontation with opposing ideas. Careful examination of others' views can lead to the readers' understanding of the logical inconsistencies in their own opinions, perspective on why they hold an opinion, and the consideration of the possibility that their opinion requires further evaluation.

Evaluating Other Opinions

To ensure that this type of examination occurs, Opposing Viewpoints books present all types of opinions. Prominent spokespeople on different sides of each issue as well as well-known professionals from many disciplines challenge the reader. An additional goal of the series is to provide a forum for other, less known, or even unpopular viewpoints. The opinion of an ordinary person who has had to make the decision to cut off life support from a terminally ill relative, for example, may be just as valuable and provide just as much insight as a medical ethicist's professional opinion. The editors have two additional purposes in including these less known views. One, the editors encourage readers to respect others' opinions—even when not enhanced by professional credibility. It is only by reading or listening to and objectively evaluating others' ideas that one can determine whether they are worthy of consideration. Two, the inclusion of such viewpoints encourages the important critical thinking skill of objectively evaluating an author's credentials and bias. This evaluation will illuminate an author's reasons for taking a particular stance on an issue and will aid in readers' evaluation of the author's ideas.

It is our hope that these books will give readers a deeper understanding of the issues debated and an appreciation of the complexity of even seemingly simple issues when good and honest people disagree. This awareness is particularly important in a democratic society such as ours in which people enter into public debate to determine the common good. Those with whom one disagrees should not be regarded as enemies but rather as people whose views deserve careful examination and may shed light on one's own.

Thomas Jefferson once said that "difference of opinion leads to inquiry, and inquiry to truth." Jefferson, a broadly educated man, argued that "if a nation expects to be ignorant and free . . . it expects what never was and never will be." As individuals and as a nation, it is imperative that we consider the opinions of others and examine them with skill and discernment. The Opposing Viewpoints Series is intended to help readers achieve this goal.

David L. Bender and Bruno Leone,
Founders

Introduction

"While it appears that the estimates of autism may be overdiagnosed, the incidence of [Asperger syndrome] is actually underdiagnosed."

Susan Ashley,
founder and director of Ashley's
Children's Psychology Center and
author of *The Asperger's Answer Book:
The Top 275 Questions Parents Ask*

"We have to make sure not everybody who is a little odd gets a diagnosis of autism or Asperger."

David J. Kupfer,
professor of psychiatry at the
University of Pittsburgh
and chair of the *DSM-V
(Diagnostic and Statistical Manual
of Mental Disorders)* Task Force

Falling under the umbrella of autism spectrum disorder (ASD), Asperger syndrome (AS) was first described in 1944. It is named after Austrian physician Hans Asperger, who observed that four boys in his practice had normal intelligence and language abilities but exhibited autistic traits: a lack of empathy, poor or absent nonverbal communication skills, clumsiness, and restricted patterns of behaviors or interests. However, his findings were not recognized until 1981, when English psychiatrist Lorna Wing published an academic paper, *Asperger's Syndrome: A Clinical Account*, introducing the term. In 1994, the American Psychiatric Association (APA) added AS to the fourth edition of its *Diagnostic and Statistical*

Manual of Mental Disorders (DSM-IV), the standard classification of mental disorders used in clinical settings and research.

There are several distinctions between AS and autism. Normal cognitive development is a primary marker; to be diagnosed with Asperger, the child must have at least average intelligence. In fact, it is labeled as "high-functioning autism" by many psychiatrists. Unlike with autism, there are no speech delays, but the use of language is typically different. "Speech patterns may be unusual, lack inflection or have a rhythmic nature, or it may be formal but too loud or high pitched,"[1] states the Autism Society. Difficulty with semantics is also apparent, and figures of speech are taken at face value. Furthermore, individuals with AS are not unresponsive as many autistic people are. But they do not learn etiquette or social cues, including eye contact, facial expressions, and body language. "Children with Asperger's Disorder may not understand the subtleties of language, such as irony and humor, or they may not understand the give-and-take nature of a conversation," adds the Autism Society.

The prevalence of Asperger is not fully researched, though some findings have been presented. It is estimated to affect 2.6 per 1,000 people and is found in all socioeconomic, ethnic, and age groups. Boys are four times more likely than girls to have the disorder. And with the absence of speech delays, AS is usually not recognized until the age of five or six. "Some of these children develop additional psychiatric symptoms and disorders in adolescence and adulthood,"[2] notes the National Institute of Neurological Disorders and Stroke. These may include depression, anxiety, obsessive-compulsive disorder, and Tourette syndrome.

Consequently, one major concern is that the disorder is often overlooked and underdiagnosed. "Asperger's syndrome is a hidden disability," asserts Paul Roud, a clinical psychologist and adjustment counselor. He cautions that reactions to individuals with it, particularly among children and adolescents, are prone to be "insensitive and even brutal" because the disability is "hidden and misunderstood."[3] Numerous experts point out that underdiagnosis is a problem facing many individuals affected by Asperger, resulting in the lack of treatment and dismissals of behavioral disorders altogether. "Considered by many to be a high functioning type of autism, it can cause major problems in a person's life. But most of the time, the problems are simply attributed to being an odd personality,"[4] asserts Ed Beckham, a psychologist in private practice. And because it is thought to mainly occur in boys, the failure of therapists to identify AS in girls is another concern. "Girls are not being picked up because there is still a stereotyped view of what Asperger's is, which is based entirely on how boys present with the condition," contends Judith Gould, director of the National Autistic Society's Lorna Wing Centre for Autism. "Professionals are not up to speed in knowing how girls present," she states.[5]

On the other hand, AS is criticized for having ambiguous diagnostic criteria and thus being overdiagnosed. "Currently, with the loosening of the diagnosis of Asperger, children and adults who are shy and timid, who have quirky interests like train schedules and baseball statistics, and who have trouble relating to their peers—but who have no language-acquisition problems—are placed on the autism spectrum," writes psychiatrist Paul Steinberg in the *New York Times*. He warns that children with social disabilities—not autism—are misplaced into education programs or schools for autistic children, leading to "lower self-esteem and poorer social development."[6] Such issues have prompted the APA to make the controversial vote to eliminate it from the fifth edition of the *DSM* (published in 2013) as a stand-alone diagnosis. "Our aim is to acknowledge the widespread consensus that Asperger syndrome is part of the autism spectrum, to clean up a currently hard-to-implement and contradictory diagnostic schema, and to do away with distinctions that are made idiosyncratically and unreliably across different diagnostic centers and clinicians,"[7] maintains Francesca Happé, a professor of cognitive neuroscience at King's College London. While the term remains accepted and used by many professionals, it is speculated that the change may hurt the Asperger community—its members proudly call themselves "aspies." According to AspergersAdvice.org, "Many people fear they will be viewed differently if seen as 'autistic' instead of having AS as well as those who fear the unique culture and identity, which has grown around the AS diagnosis, may be affected."[8]

A relatively new diagnosis that has recently grown in public awareness, Asperger and its removal from the *DSM-V* underscores the current challenges to validity, assessments, prevalence, and policies facing behavioral disorders. *Opposing Viewpoints: Behavioral Disorders* explores these and related topics in the following chapters: Are Behavioral Disorders a Serious Problem?, What Factors Contribute to Behavioral Disorders?, How Should Behavioral Disorders Be Treated?, and What Policies Will Best Address the Challenges of Behavioral Disorders? The range of analyses, research, and perspectives in this anthology represent the questions and complexities surrounding abnormal human behavior.

Notes

1. Autism Society, "Asperger's Syndrome." www.autism-society.org/about-autism/aspergers-syndrome (accessed February 22, 2013).
2. National Institute of Neurological Disorders and Stroke, "Asperger Syndrome Fact Sheet," February 4, 2013. www.ninds.nih.gov/disorders/asperger/detail_asperger.htm.
3. Quoted in *Teaching Tolerance*, "Meeting Mathew," Fall 2012.
4. Ed Beckham, "Asperger—the Most Underdiagnosed Disorder?," Dr. Beckham's Blog, December 22, 2010. http://drbeckham.blogspot.com/2010/12/most-underdiagnosed-disorder.html.

5. Quoted in Amelia Hill, "Doctors Are 'Failing to Spot Asperger's' in Girls," *The Guardian* (Manchester, UK), April 11, 2009.

6. Paul Steinberg, "Asperger's History of Overdiagnosis," *New York Times*, January 31, 2012. www.nytimes.com/2012/02/01/opinion/aspergers-history-of-over-diagnosis.html?ref= opinion.

7. Francesca Happé, "Why Fold Asperger Syndrome into Autism Spectrum Disorder in the DSM-5?," Simon Foundation Autism Research Initiative, March 29, 2011. https://sfari.org/news-and-opinion/viewpoint/2011/why-fold-asperger -syndrome-into-autism-spectrum-disorder-in-the-dsm-5.

8. Asperger's Advice, "DSM-V—What Does It All Mean?," January 16, 2013. www.aspergersadvice.org/dsm-v-what -does-it-all-mean.

OPPOSING
VIEWPOINTS®
SERIES

CHAPTER 1

Are Behavioral Disorders
a Serious Problem?

Chapter Preface

About 4 percent of adults are estimated to have attention-deficit/hyperactivity disorder (ADHD). "The symptoms of ADHD in adults are the same as those in children, but they manifest somewhat differently in adults," states Patrick E. Clarke of the US Food and Drug Administration's Office of Communications. "Adults with ADHD may have poor time-management skills, have trouble with multitasking, become restless with downtime, and avoid activities that require sustained concentration," he explains. Additionally, the individual must have a history of behavioral issues such as impulsivity and constantly interrupting or intruding on others. "A diagnosis of ADHD in an adult is only given when it's known that some of the symptoms were present early in childhood," Clarke notes, adding, "usually under the age of seven."

Some experts suggest that adult ADHD is underdiagnosed. For example, some research indicates that 60 to 90 percent of children do not outgrow the symptoms as adults. "That means if an ADHD diagnosis is missed in childhood, the individual might need treatment when he or she gets older," observes Christine S. Mover, a staff writer for *American Medical News*. Some professionals maintain that many of these individuals do not receive the proper medical help. "Adult ADHD is chronically misunderstood," claims Roslyn Ross Steeler, a psychotherapist and social worker, adding that "a multitude of patients have spent years spinning their wheels in psychotherapy without having had their ADD [attention-deficit disorder] diagnosed or treated."

Other experts, however, view adult ADHD with skepticism and do not see it as a valid diagnosis. "Definitions of adult ADHD include numerous aspects of mental functioning and behaviour that are not usually examined in children—such as mood swings, irritability, stress intolerance, anger, and risk taking—and play down central features of childhood ADHD such as hyperactivity," argue psychiatrists Joanna Moncrieff and Sami Timimi in the *British Medical Journal*. Indeed, they assert that identifying and treating the disorder in older patients is driven by profit motives. "The speed with which the diagnosis of adult ADHD has been accepted, its vagueness, and the lack of evidence for the usefulness of specific treatments indicate that it is the latest of several medical and psychiatric fashions, which have been fuelled by the interests of the drugs industry," Moncrieff and Timimi contend. Furthermore, many people—particularly college students—are accused of faking the symptoms of ADHD in order to be prescribed medication, which is a stimulant that can enhance performance and become addictive. In a 2011 survey, 38 percent of physicians suspected patients of feigning the disorder to obtain prescriptions.

The authors of the viewpoints in the following chapter debate the legitimacy and extent of ADHD and other behavioral disorders.

> "ADHD ... made our above-average child seem like someone who was mentally challenged."

Attention-Deficit/Hyperactivity Disorder Is a Real Disease

Zinnia Jones

Zinnia Jones is a writer, video blogger, and mother of a son with attention-deficit/hyperactivity disorder (ADHD). In the following viewpoint, she insists that ADHD may be misdiagnosed in some children, but is a real condition with detrimental effects in others. Drawing from experiences with her son's disorder, Jones disagrees that the diagnosis medicalizes normal childhood behavior and that medication is unnecessarily prescribed in place of environmental changes. She maintains that her son struggled with severe symptoms of ADHD—initially misdiagnosed as being mentally handicapped—and did not show significant improvement until he was medicated. All forms of treatment and support should be available to children properly diagnosed with ADHD, Jones concludes, and medication should not be condemned out of hand.

As you read, consider the following questions:

1. What is Jones's view of theories that ADHD is not real?

2. What examples does the author provide of her son's struggles with ADHD at school and home?

3. As described by Jones, what can the lack of treatment for ADHD lead to?

A lot of people seem to have the idea that attention deficit hyperactivity disorder is something less than a real condition. Many have claimed that the diagnosis of ADHD pathologizes what's actually normal childhood behavior, or that it's presented as a problem in order to sell a solution in the form of unnecessary medication with unknown long-term effects. Others say that ADHD is real but overdiagnosed, and medication is used where changes to the child's environment would be more appropriate. Most recently, the *New York Times* reported on a doctor who prescribed ADHD medication to children who are struggling in school, regardless of whether they actually have ADHD. He believes that the school system is poorly suited to children, but that people are unwilling to make changes on a systemic level, and so they resort to medicating their children.

The problem is that many of these folk theories about the reality, causes and proper treatment of ADHD are mostly, in my opinion, nonsense, perpetuated by people who think they've uncovered some grand conspiracy but have very little understanding of what they're talking about.

Our 9-year-old son has ADHD, and he takes medication for it. His mother has ADHD, his father has ADHD, and his younger brother sometimes appears to have symptoms of ADHD—although this can be largely indistinguishable from the typical range of toddler behavior. And anyone who believes that ADHD is a hoax or can be addressed solely by environmental changes should really try spending some time with our son when he's unmedicated.

While it's certainly possible that children have been inappropriately diagnosed with ADHD in some circumstances, this does nothing to show that ADHD does not exist in other children. This also isn't a matter of making an exclusive choice between either medication or alternative means of support. There's no reason why we can't use everything at our disposal to treat this. And while the side effects of medication always need to be taken into account, it's also crucial to consider the effects of withholding treatment that works.

We waited for as long as possible before looking into medication for our son. We explored every other option that was available to us. He had a specialized plan at school and extra tutoring, and he still does. We worked closely with him every day to help him understand his work, and we gave him extra practice in every subject. And *it wasn't enough.*

Environment Was Not the Problem

This was not just an instance of a child chafing against the unreasonable constraints of standardized education. His environment was not the problem, and shaping his environment around him would have meant letting him flounder. This was a second-grader who would often spend three hours trying to complete a single sheet of simple addition with the help of two adults. This was a child who had to be reminded a dozen times before he would even remember how to complete a basic task like setting the table, let alone actually getting it done. This was a kid who could not stop himself from talking, yelling, and running wildly around the house. His insomnia would keep him up all night, doing nothing but talking to himself in bed, until he was so tired that he fell asleep almost every day in school. His teachers would make him sit through 40 minutes of reading class, 15 minutes of recess, and 50 more minutes of science class just trying to get him to write a single sentence.

His eyes would glaze over halfway through trying his best to add 5 and 4, when he lost track of what he was doing and had to start over for the third time. He would stumble through trying to read short sentences and couldn't tell us what they actually meant even after we read them back to him. He continually failed to be influenced by incentives or even understand their purpose. He forgot to bring home his work, and he didn't turn it in when it was finished. He would burst into tears every day when trying to do his homework. He told us he was "the worst kid ever" and that he wanted to kill himself. This was a child who was going to be held back a grade, *again*. And he knew that he had a serious problem. He did not like how he was, and he did not want to be like this. He just wanted to be good, and he *couldn't*, no matter how hard he tried.

"Over-diagnosed"

His instructors and evaluators refused to believe that he could have ADHD, because they thought it was "over-diagnosed." They laughed at my partner when she suggested it, even when she told them that his father had been successfully treated for ADHD. Instead, they claimed he was mentally handicapped, and that was why he was consistently performing more slowly than the other children. We knew that couldn't be the case, because in those brief moments when we could get him to focus, he *could* understand his work. Something was just getting in the way. Only after intelligence tests found him to be above average did his teachers admit that ADHD was a possibility.

We had already figured this out, and we *still* didn't want to have to medicate him. We were worried about the long-term effects, too. We didn't want him to have to rely on medication instead of developing coping strategies. But we were wrong. Eventually, we had to recognize that this constant pain was not encouraging him to develop coping strategies. It was only making him miserable. This wasn't helping him to grow—it was destroying him. Those who criticize parents for supposedly "taking the easy way out" when they have their children treated for ADHD have made the mistake of thinking that

The Problems of Adult ADHD

Though one third of adults with ADHD [attention-deficit/hyperactivity disorder] may progress satisfactorily into their adult years, another one third continues to experience some level of problems, while the final third continues to experience and often develops significant problems related to ADHD and other comorbid conditions. By combining a number of outcome studies, it is reasonable to conclude that 10% to 20% of adults with histories of ADHD experience few problems. Sixty percent continue to demonstrate symptoms of ADHD and experience social, academic and emotional problems to at least a mild to moderate degree and 10% to 30% develop antisocial problems in addition to their continued difficulty with ADHD and other comorbidities. Many of these negative outcomes are linked to the continuity, severity and persistence of ADHD symptoms. Though males may experience more problems with disruptive and aggressive behavior, females with ADHD appear to suffer equally in all other arenas of life.

Sam Goldstein, foreword to ADHD in Adults
by Susan Young and Jessica Bramham, 2007.

struggle must always be virtuous. They want to believe there must be some great payoff in proportion to all the trouble. But sometimes there's not. In reality, his ongoing struggles weren't good for any of us. We had to accept that when it came to the well-being of our son, it wasn't our principles that mattered—it was the results.

Has his medication been a cure-all? Of course not, and this was by no means an excuse to stop helping him. He still gets all the support he needs from his family and from his school. The difference is that now, it's actually working. Instead of running just to stay in place and still falling behind, this makes progress possible. He remembers to bring his work home and [to] turn it in. He can finish his homework on his own without requiring constant attention, and he gets it right. He doesn't fall asleep in school, and when he stays up late, he actually chooses to read books. He can focus and tell us what the sentences mean. He listens to us, he can control himself, and he can behave himself. And he smiles so much more! He's happy now, he's less anxious, and his attitude toward school has improved remarkably considering how difficult it had been for him. He's passing instead of failing, because he finally has the basic abilities that are required to learn and succeed.

Putting Options on an Equal Footing

The inertia of the status quo often gives it a certain privilege in people's minds. They set higher standards of justification for switching to an alternative than they would for simply staying on the present course. But when we put our options on an equal footing and considered them fairly, we could not justify depriving him of the treatment that would actually help. This isn't just a matter of how it's affecting him now. When ADHD isn't properly treated, it can lead to higher rates of substance abuse, anxiety, depression, dropping out, car accidents, unwanted pregnancies, STDs [sexually transmitted diseases], unemployment, and everything else you might expect to result from being chronically unable to think clearly. And we're not willing to stand by and watch him fail over and over while we try to find alternative treatments when we already have one that works.

This was not our first choice, and if other means were sufficient to control his symptoms, we wouldn't have chosen to medicate him. But as of right now, this is not possible. Do we enjoy paying for expensive medication? No, but there is *abso-*

lutely no way I can regard it as some kind of scam. The value to our entire family has been incalculable. ADHD had made our above-average child seem like someone who was mentally challenged. This is what finally worked to undo that, and I could *never* expect other parents to forgo a treatment that's had such a transformative effect.

Regardless of what anyone else may think, this is a personal decision to be made by the family based on their situation and their needs, and I don't find it at all appropriate to issue blanket condemnations of medication for ADHD when this may be exactly what someone's child needs. Everyone wants what's best for kids, and certainly nobody wants what's worse for them. But when people are unclear on how to achieve this, their ignorance can lead them to conclusions that fail to respect the reality of what these children are dealing with. We would know—we've been there.

| "*There is no such thing as ADHD as a disease.*"

Attention-Deficit/Hyperactivity Disorder Is Not a Disease

Fred Baughman, as told to The Mark News

In the following viewpoint, Fred Baughman argues that attention-deficit/hyperactivity disorder (ADHD) is a fraudulent diagnosis created by the psychiatry and pharmaceutical industries to generate profits. Lacking any sort of gross, microscopic, or chemical abnormality, ADHD is not a physical disease, Baughman contends, and children normally exhibit its symptoms— such as impulsivity and disruptive behavior—at some stage in their youth. The invention of ADHD to market drugs not only stigmatizes children but puts their lives at risk with dangerous medications, Baughman insists.

Based in El Cajon, California, Fred Baughman is a child neurologist and fellow of the American Academy of Neurology.

As you read, consider the following questions:

1. As stated by the author, how much was spent on ADHD drugs in 2010?

2. What does Baughman call psychiatrists' claims that their diagnoses are chemical imbalances?

3. What caused several deaths of children in Canada in 2005, according to the author?

Some 5.4 million children in the United States have been diagnosed with attention-deficit hyperactivity disorder, or ADHD, with two-thirds of them taking psychiatric drugs. Sales of ADHD drugs reached $1.2 billion in 2010, a demand level so high that the U.S. is experiencing an ADHD drug shortage. But an increasingly vocal contingent of psychiatric experts is speaking up against diagnosing children with ADHD, arguing it is a non-existent condition drummed up by pharmaceutical companies to increase sales.

A Marketing Strategy

The Mark News: What makes you convinced that ADHD is not a real disease?
Fred Baughman: During my time in practice, I've authored papers and discovered real diseases and so on. Psychiatry in 1948 was distinguished from neurology. Neurology is the specialty dealing with physical and organic diseases of the brain and nervous system. Psychiatry is the specialty dealing with emotional and behavioural things which are not actual, physical diseases—things like depression, anxiety, panic, and so on.

Insofar as ADHD is concerned, it seems clear that in the '50s, as the first psychiatric drugs came to market, that psychiatry—in cahoots with the pharmaceutical industry—came upon the market strategy of, "Well, we'll call these things 'diseases.'" And the prototypical invented disease was called ADHD.

It was initially in a 1970 congressional hearing in the U.S. that psychiatrists appeared and testified that, what was then called hyper kinetic disorder or minimal brain dysfunction, was a disease that needed diagnosing by a physician, and as a disease it justified the use of drugs to treat it. So that was the official beginning of ADHD in particular and of psychiatric diagnoses in general as being due to a disease of the brain. In every case, they say there's a subtle chemical imbalance in the brain, which of course they never have a means of diagnosing in life and have never in scientific literature authored proof that there is in fact a disease. And yet they are allowed by [the U.S.] Food and Drug Administration to say that there is a chemical imbalance and that the drugs balance the imbalance.

So it's been a market strategy. This lie has been allowed to be published by the drug industry and by psychiatry, by our regulatory agencies, specifically the Food and Drug Administration. So that's where we are today.

All physicians learn in medical school that a disease is a physical abnormality. When you go to your physician, they may see a rash or they may find something microscopically abnormal, such as cancer cells. Then there are a lot of chemical diseases—diabetes being the best known. There are about a hundred examples of inborn errors of metabolism or body chemistry. These can all be tested for, they've all been proven, and they exist in the scientific literature—whereas there is not a single psychiatric diagnosis that exists in the scientific literature of the world.

In 2008, I was counselling a young father from Kingston, Ontario, who was in a divorce situation, and the mother insisted the children be seen by psychiatrists, and the psychiatrist had made a number of diagnoses and had this one boy on large amounts of about five or six different types of medication. I helped the father author a letter to Health Canada asking where—in the case of ADHD or any psychiatric diagnosis—there is proof of a gross or microscopic abnormality.

This gentleman got a letter back from the director-general of Health Canada saying there is no gross, microscopic, or chemical abnormality in any psychiatric diagnosis; there is no objective way of verifying a psychiatric diagnosis as a disease.

That's why psychiatry's claims that their diagnoses are chemical imbalances is nothing but a lie and a deception. And yet, because of their financial might on the world scene, no one will challenge them. They have friends bought and paid for in government and in all of the governmental health-care agencies.

Here in the States, as of 2007, the Centers for Disease Control announced that 5.4 million U.S. schoolchildren five to 17 years old had ADHD. And you can be sure that they have all been on ADHD drugs, which are, for the most part, amphetamines, which are known to be addictive, dangerous, deadly.

I've heard estimates of 20 per cent of schoolchildren in the U.S. with a psych diagnosis and who were on psych drugs. It's exploding, it's increasing all the time.

A Complete Fraud

Is the issue that we're overmedicating ourselves, or that ADHD is not real?
When it's a total fraud, you don't call it overmedicating. There is no such thing as ADHD as a disease, so there is never justification for it. It's a total fraud.
What is there to gain from diagnosing children with ADHD?
Ritalin has passed $1 billion a year in sales. Ritalin is no longer the top ADHD drug in the U.S. I think Adderall, which is made up of amphetamines, passed Ritalin a few years ago in market share.

It's a complete fraud, they've invented diseases for which their drugs are a cure. The rate of diagnosing ADHD has been going up by a million a year in the U.S. This is a market strategy.

The book *Selling Sickness: How the World's Biggest Pharmaceutical Companies Are Turning Us All into Patients* [by Ray Moynihan and Alan Cassels] talks generally about inventing

"We'll discuss your misbehavior in a moment Billy,
but in the meantime, why don't you help yourself
to a nice piece of candy?"

© Loren Fishman/lfin266/cartoonstock.com.

diseases for which to sell drugs. In the foreword of that book, the authors quote the former president of Merck Pharmaceutical Co., Henry Gadsden, who once said he was anxious to find ways to market his products to normal people, just like the Wrigley chewing gum people did. This was kind of an after-the-fact confession they were trying to market drugs to normal people, and calling all psychological dilemmas diseases for which they needed a pill. This was the strategy.

It's almost unimaginable, it's almost unthinkable that this has been going on, but that's exactly what's been going on.

Behaviors, Not Diseases

How would you diagnose a child that was considered to have ADHD?

Look at the criteria that are used to call a child ADHD. They talk out of turn, they don't sit still, they wiggle around too much in their seats, they are impulsive, disorderly, and so on. It's a bunch of behaviours that are seen in just about every child at some stage of their life. This is by design; they have taken kind of irritating, bothersome, disruptive behaviours in children and have kind of cobbled them together and called it a disease.

They get a lot of parents to buy it because a lot of parents are now busy with their job in the workforce and there's no longer a full-time parent in the home, and so, "Here's why Johnny or Janey is such an irritant to me, they've got ADHD." It takes the pressure entirely off the parent for not being a presence and for not being there full-time to mould the behaviour of the child, and they're calling these behaviours a disease and saying we've got a pill for it. That's very seductive. That's a far more appealing analysis than, "Gee, you're divorced, there's no one in the home to discipline the child real time," and so on.

These are not diseases, they are behaviours. Today, you hang a psychiatric label on a child, you surely stigmatize the child and these drugs are exceedingly dangerous. In 2005, there were several deaths in Canada of young children from Adderall. It was temporarily taken off the market, but then the power of the industry won out and Adderall's back on the market. Pure amphetamines.

> *"Bipolar children . . . desperately need attention for this poorly understood and ill-treated disorder."*

Bipolar Disorder in Children Is a Serious Problem

Mani Pavuluri

Mani Pavuluri is a child psychiatry professor at the University of Illinois at Chicago and author of What Works for Bipolar Kids: Help and Hope for Parents. *In the following viewpoint Pavuluri states that bipolar disorder occurs in children, which is not widely recognized. She explains that earlier in her research she gave a combination of other disorders as a diagnosis for these children, but it did not address their elated mood, grandiosity, and excitability. But when she began to treat their condition like bipolar disorder in adults, Pavuluri claims that she saw improvement. Childhood bipolar disorder is not fully understood and the label is imperfect, but it is better to help these children now through available treatments, insists the author.*

As you read, consider the following questions:

1. How do medical professionals react to potential cases of childhood bipolar disorder, in Pavuluri's opinion?

Mani Pavuluri, "Yes, Bipolar Disorder Does Occur in Children," *What Works for Bipolar Kids: Help and Hope for Parents.* New York: Guilford Press, 2008. Copyright © 2008 by Guilford Publications, Inc. All rights reserved. Reproduced by permission.

2. As told by the author, how did the child bipolar disorder begin to take shape in research?

3. What debate continues about bipolar disorder among mental health experts, as noted by Pavuluri?

Jeremy walks in, wearing a broad smile. He chats garrulously with my staff. He is extremely hyper and starts playing with all the other patients in the waiting area, making rules and bossing them around. Seeing me, he runs up and twists my arm hard as we shake hands. He bursts into laughter as I pull my hand away. His mom, who looks tired and helpless, tells us Jeremy hardly slept the night before. He is chirpy and giggly, talking like a super-express train. He agrees to be videotaped, and my staff goes to get the equipment, but as soon as the camera is set up, his mood changes completely. He starts to direct the filming, then suddenly gets irritable and goes out of control, knocking over the equipment and swearing nonstop.

A Few More Examples

This is a real example from my clinic. Although somewhat dramatic, stories like these are hardly isolated incidents among bipolar children. Here are a few more examples of things that our patients said or did while in our clinic:

- John (age 10) lifted my research assistants up in his arms; he even attempted to pick up men twice his size and hug strangers, although he would startle and yell if anyone touched him.

- Cindy (age 6) threw herself onto the floor in the hospital corridor and refused to move or get up. She screamed incessantly and turned red in a rage for a half hour before getting blood drawn.

- Jared (age 11) touched everything in sight, talking constantly about things that seemed to have nothing to do with what he was exploring and ricocheting from one topic to the next. "I was thinking that there was this hamster that looked into a mirror and thought there was another hamster and he ran into the mirror!" he said, then laughed hysterically before darting off to another part of my office and telling a story about the time he had "saved" his brother from a dog with "teeth at least a foot long."

- Sylvia (age 9) hid testing materials in our lab in the bottom of a Kleenex box, locked my staff out of the office, threw testing materials away, and jumped up and down in the garbage can.

- Andy (age 7) saw a bird fly against the window of his third-floor playroom and land dazed on the roof below. He climbed out the window and onto the roof in an attempt to help the bird. When his mother retrieved him safely and asked him what he was doing, he responded, "I can fly." His mother reminded him that people can't fly, and he said, "Then God would save me."

- Hannah (age 8) declared, "I'm going to marry you and make you my pretty, pretty princess." She was provocative and overfriendly for a first meeting.

- In the course of 15 minutes during the diagnostic evaluation, Asaad (age 5) went from laughter to yelling and turning red, then broke down crying, unable to articulate his problems given his very young age.

- Joe (age 12) let out a torrent of taunts and criticisms, talking so fast that he was almost incoherent, yelling constantly, rationalizing his anger, and calling his mother a "moron" who had "no brains" as if he were a viciously angry ex-husband. . . .

One Size Does Not Fit All

Even medical professionals have varying reactions to these types of cameos. Either they think these are accurate depictions of childhood bipolar disorder, or they believe that these are difficult behaviors not specific to bipolar disorder, or they dismiss them all as not really bipolar disorder. One parent was often told there was no such "animal" as early-onset or childhood bipolar disorder, and because she was in the mental health field she was accused of "looking for a problem that simply isn't there."

Let me take a minute to clarify how you should view the behaviors portrayed in these very brief stories. The complex emotional turbulence and havoc caused by these children is obvious and dramatic, but parents and professionals should realize that one size does *not* fit all—in other words, no one description captures all the typical bipolar diagnostic symptoms. [The] child might have the "classic symptoms," which easily lead to diagnosis, and/or some difficult behaviors, like those described above, which occur more rarely but are definitely associated with the disorder. Because at our clinic we treat hundreds of bipolar children and research their brains and cognitive function, we recognize the wide range of symptoms that can lead to a diagnosis of pediatric bipolar disorder. We think in terms of treating a spectrum of problems related to wiring in the brain that cause dysfunction, rather than just hanging a label on a child based on a diagnosis.

Unfortunately, not everyone recognizes the diagnosis, and there is still a lot of controversy over the label. . . . Make no mistake about it; bipolar disorder does exist in children. The answers to the questions [about the] condition aren't always simple or definitive, but they are becoming clearer as brain imaging and clinical research continue to reveal new and useful insights about childhood bipolar disorder each year.

What Is Childhood Bipolar Disorder?

Bipolar disorder is a mood disorder characterized by swings between the opposite and extreme emotional states of mania and depression. The simplest way to put it would be to say that people who have bipolar disorder are sometimes much more "up"—excited, energetic, optimistic, and so forth—than the rest of us and other times much more "down"—that is, sad, dejected, lethargic, and hopeless. But this condition is actually much more complex than that definition implies, and that's why the term "bipolar" is more commonly used today than the older "manic depression"—because it is thought more accurately to reflect the disorder's cyclical nature and the wide variety of symptoms that accompany its two poles (the "bi") of ups and downs. A person suffering from bipolar disorder will not necessarily appear to be energized and happy at one time and visibly sorrowful at another. A person experiencing either mania or depression can seem mainly highly irritable, and the line between the two mood poles isn't always very clear, especially in children.

Differences in the way children manifest bipolar disorder, in fact, started to take shape in the mid-1990s, when new research opened the door to our present understanding. Various researchers looked at the disorder from different angles, each one focusing on a different symptom or dimension as the hallmark of the disease: one focused on irritability, which is a common reason for families to seek treatment for their children; another focused on grandiosity and elated mood; and another stuck to the classic symptoms of mood states that fluctuated from mania to depression similarly to late-adolescent-onset/adult bipolar disorder.

The Debate Continues

In order to come to a consensus, in 2001, the National Institute of Mental Health (NIMH) convened two Research Roundtables with experts in the field, which produced a general

Childhood Bipolar Disorder Is Real

The concern regarding a diagnosis of bipolar disorder in children was inflamed after a two-year-old reportedly died from overmedication with drugs prescribed for bipolar disorder. *Frontline's* coverage of childhood bipolar disorder, titled "The Medicated Child," only fueled public dismay regarding this diagnosis and its treatment by the psychiatric community. Unfortunately, as more attention is focused on misdiagnosis or overmedication for bipolar disorder in children, less attention is paid to children who do exhibit symptoms of mania and depression. The film *Boy Interrupted* documents the life of a boy with bipolar disorder from childhood to adolescence and captures his day-to-day struggle at home, with friends, and at school. After a long period on and then off lithium, he commits suicide, jumping from his bedroom window. Some findings indicate that children with bipolar disorder have a high rate of suicidal behavior and more severe features of bipolar illness than do adults.

Lisa Hermsen, Manic Minds:
Mania's Mad History and Its Neuro-Future, *2011.*

agreement about the main types of bipolar disorder, one based on a narrow definition consisting of the classic symptoms described above and the other a broader definition that encompasses a wide range of symptoms, including severe irritability, "affective storms," mood lability, and severe temper outbursts, falling short of the full set of symptoms or without clearly defined mood cycles. Debate continues between various schools of thought, with some believing that the criteria are being applied too broadly and others feeling that a narrow definition, "the middle cut," leaves out too many children who should be helped.

A Distinct Disorder in Children

I, too, erred on the side of caution in diagnosis when I came from Australia to the United States in the late 1990s. I used to diagnose what we now think of as childhood bipolar disorder as attention-deficit/hyperactivity disorder (ADHD) (as children with bipolar disorder are hyperactive and distractible) + oppositional defiant disorder (ODD) (as they are irritable and difficult but short of conduct problems) + major depression (as they had mixed depressive symptoms). This diagnosis still did not address these children's elated mood, grandiosity, excitability and exuberance, creative and excessive productivity, flights of ideas and pressured speech, sleep difficulties, or hypersexuality. We could not control their emotional dysregulation. Like most of my colleagues, I treated these children with stimulants or antidepressants, with poor results. It was like the fable of the blind men trying to describe an elephant—we defined the problem based on the part we were touching at the time.

I spent significant amounts of time investigating the syndrome to understand it better. I began to attract patients from all over the country and abroad, and in the course of treating them, a pattern emerged. I saw that the mood fluctuations weren't just a matter of temperament. They worsened with age. In addition, the symptoms and cycles didn't behave exactly like bipolar disorder in adults. Two big things convinced me that this was a distinct disorder that manifested itself in children uniquely: (1) treating it as simply ADHD, depression, or a combination of the two did not do the trick; it was much more complicated than any of these other conditions; and (2) treating it like adult bipolar disorder seemed to help these children, although there were some important differences owing to brain development and their youth when symptoms began.

I felt compelled to do something to help bipolar children who desperately need attention for this poorly understood and ill-treated disorder. Although we don't yet fully under-stand the disorder or its causes, we must start treating it while our understanding of the brain and nervous system continues to evolve. Rather than being submerged in debate, we must apply these scientific findings to making a difference *now* for kids in the real world and not keep them waiting! I believe it is better to embrace an imperfect label and do what's right by treating these suffering kids.

"*The problem is, this apparent [child-hood bipolar] epidemic isn't real.*"

Bipolar Disorder Is Widely Misdiagnosed in Children

Jon Ronson

Childhood bipolar disorder is not epidemic, maintains Jon Ronson in the following viewpoint. It is diagnosed with a superficial checklist of behaviors—which include normal behaviors—created with the agenda of psychiatrists, he contends. Furthermore, Ronson claims, the epidemic has been perpetuated by the profit-seeking pharmaceutical industry and childhood bipolar disorder advocates. As more kids are diagnosed with bipolar disorder, the author concludes, the more they are prescribed unnecessary medications with adverse side effects.

Jon Ronson is a London writer and documentary filmmaker and the author of The Psychopath Test.

As you read, consider the following questions:

1. How have officially recognized disorders been created, according to Ronson?

2. What is Allen Frances's view of childhood bipolar disorder?

3. What example does Ronson provide of the dangers of medicating children for bipolar disorder?

There's a children's picture book in the US called *Brandon and the Bipolar Bear*. Brandon and his bear sometimes fly into unprovoked rages. Sometimes they're silly and overexcited. A nice doctor tells them they are ill, and gives them medicine that makes them feel much better.

The thing is, if Brandon were a real child, he would have just been misdiagnosed with bipolar disorder.

Also known as manic depression, this serious condition, involving dramatic mood swings, is increasingly being recorded in American children. And a vast number of them are being medicated for it.

The problem is, this apparent epidemic isn't real. "Bipolar emerges from late adolescence," says Ian Goodyer, a professor in the department of psychiatry at the University of Cambridge who studies child and adolescent depression. "It is very, very unlikely indeed that you'll find it in children under 7 years."

How did this strange, sweeping misdiagnosis come to pass? How did it all start? These were some of the questions I explored when researching *The Psychopath Test*, my new book about the odder corners of the "madness industry".

A Freudian Slip

The answer to the second question turned out to be strikingly simple. It was really all because of one man: Robert Spitzer.

I met Spitzer in his large, airy house in Princeton, New Jersey. In his eighties now, he remembered his childhood camping trips to upstate New York. "I'd sit in the tent, looking out, writing notes about the lady campers," he said. "Their attributes." He smiled. "I've always liked to classify people."

The trips were respite from Spitzer's "very unhappy mother". In the 1940s, the only help on offer was psychoanalysis, the Freudian-based approach of exploring the patient's unconscious. "She went from one psychoanalyst to another," said Spitzer. He watched the psychoanalysts flailing uselessly. She never got better.

Spitzer grew up to be a psychiatrist at Columbia University, New York, his dislike of psychoanalysis remaining undimmed. And then, in 1973, an opportunity to change everything presented itself.

There was a job going editing the next edition of a little-known spiral-bound booklet called *DSM—the Diagnostic and Statistical Manual of Mental Disorders*.

DSM is simply a list of all the officially recognised mental illnesses and their symptoms. Back then it was a tiny book that reflected the Freudian thinking predominant in the 1960s. It had very few pages, and very few readers.

What nobody knew when they offered Spitzer the job was that he had a plan: to try to remove human judgement from psychiatry. He would create a whole new *DSM* that would eradicate all that crass sleuthing around the unconscious; it hadn't helped his mother. Instead it would be all about checklists. Any psychiatrist could pick up the manual, and if the patient's symptoms tallied with the checklist for a particular disorder, that would be the diagnosis.

For six years Spitzer held editorial meetings at Columbia. They were chaos. The psychiatrists would yell out the names of potential new mental disorders and the checklists of their symptoms. There would be a cacophony of voices in assent or dissent—the loudest voices getting listened to the most. If Spitzer agreed with those proposing a new diagnosis, which he almost always did, he'd hammer it out instantly on an old typewriter. And there it would be, set in stone.

That's how practically every disorder you've ever heard of or been diagnosed with came to be defined. "Post-traumatic stress disorder," said Spitzer, "attention-deficit disorder, autism, anorexia nervosa, bulimia, panic disorder . . ." each with its own checklist of symptoms. Bipolar disorder was another of the newcomers. The previous edition of the *DSM* had been 134 pages, but when Spitzer's *DSM-III* appeared in 1980 it ran to 494 pages.

"Were there any proposals for mental disorders you rejected?" I asked Spitzer. "Yes," he said, "atypical child syndrome. The problem came when we tried to find out how to characterise it. I said, 'What are the symptoms?' The man proposing it replied: 'That's hard to say because the children are very atypical.'"

He paused. "And we were going to include masochistic personality disorder." He meant battered wives who stayed with their husbands. "But there were some violently opposed feminists who thought it was labelling the victim. We changed the name to self-defeating personality disorder and put it into the appendix."

DSM-III was a sensation. It sold over a million copies—many more copies than there were psychiatrists. Millions of people began using the checklists to diagnose themselves. For many it was a godsend. Something was categorically wrong with them and finally their suffering had a name. It was truly a revolution in psychiatry.

It was also a gold rush for drug companies, which suddenly had 83 new disorders they could invent medications for. "The pharmaceuticals were delighted with *DSM*," Spitzer told me, and this in turn delighted him: "I love to hear parents who say, 'It was impossible to live with him until we gave him medication and then it was [like the difference between] night and day.'"

Spitzer's successor, a psychiatrist named Allen Frances, continued the tradition of welcoming new mental disorders, with their corresponding checklists, into the fold. His *DSM-IV* came in at a mammoth 886 pages, with an extra 32 mental disorders.

Now Frances told me over the phone he felt he had made some terrible mistakes. "Psychiatric diagnoses are getting closer and closer to the boundary of normal," he said.

"Why?" I asked. "There's a societal push for conformity in all ways," he said. "There's less tolerance of difference. Maybe for some people having a label confers a sense of hope— 'previously I was laughed at but now I can talk to fellow sufferers on the internet'."

Part of the problem is the pharmaceutical industry. "It's very easy to set off a false epidemic in psychiatry," said Frances. "The drug companies have tremendous influence."

One condition that Frances considers a mistake is childhood bipolar disorder. "Kids with extreme temper tantrums are being called bipolar," he said. "Childhood bipolar takes the edge of guilt away from parents that maybe they created an oppositional child."

"So maybe the diagnosis is good?"

"No," Frances said. "And there are very good reasons why not." His main concern is that children whose behaviour only superficially matches the bipolar checklist get treated with antipsychotic drugs, which can succeed in calming them down, even if the diagnosis is wrong. These drugs can have unpleasant and sometimes dangerous side effects.

Propagating a False Epidemic

The drug companies aren't the only ones responsible for propagating this false epidemic. Patient advocacy groups can be very fiery too. The author of *Brandon and the Bipolar Bear*, Tracy Anglada, is head of a childhood bipolar advocacy group called BP Children. She emailed me that she wished me all the best with my project but she didn't want to be interviewed. If, however, I wanted to submit a completed manuscript to her, she added, she'd be happy to consider it for review.

Anglada's friend Bryna Hebert has also written a children's book: *My Bipolar, Roller Coaster, Feelings Book*. "Matt! Will you take your medicines please?" she called across the kitchen when I visited her at home in Barrington, Rhode Island. The medicines were lined up on the kitchen table. Her son Matt, 14 years old, took them straight away.

The family's nickname for baby Matt had been Mister Manic Depressive. "Because his mood would change so fast. He'd be sitting in his high chair, happy as a clam; 2 seconds later he'd be throwing things across the room. When he was 3 he'd hit and not be sorry that he hit. He was obsessed with vampires. He'd cut out bits of paper and put them into his teeth like vampire teeth and go up to strangers. Hiss hiss hiss. It was a little weird."

"Were you getting nervous?" I asked. "Yeah," said Hebert. "One day he wanted some pretzels before lunch, and I told him no. He grabbed a butcher knife and threatened me."

"How old was he?"

"Four. That was the only time he's ever done anything that extreme," she said. "Oh, he's hit his sister Jessica in the head and kicked her in the stomach."

"She's the one who punched *me* in the head," called Matt from across the room.

It was after the knife incident, Hebert said, [that] they took him to be tested. As it happened, the paediatric unit at what was then their local hospital, Massachusetts General, was run by Joseph Biederman, the doyen [dean] of childhood bipolar disorder. According to a 2008 article in the *San Francisco Chronicle*, "Biederman's influence is so great that when he merely mentions a drug during a presentation, tens of thousands of children will end up taking it." Biederman has said bipolar disorder can start, "from the moment the child opens his eyes".

"When they were testing Matt he was under the table, he was on top of the table," said Hebert. "We went through all these checklists. One of Dr Biederman's colleagues said," We really think "Matt meets the criteria in the *DSM* for bipolar disorder."

That was 10 years ago and Matt has been medicated ever since. So has his sister Jessica, who was also diagnosed by Biederman's people as bipolar. "We've been through a million medications," said Hebert. "There's weight gain. Tics. Irritability. Sedation. They work for a couple of years then they stop working."

Hebert was convinced her children were bipolar, and I wasn't going to swoop into a stranger's home for an afternoon and tell her they were normal. That would have been incredibly patronising and offensive. Plus, as the venerable child psychiatrist David Shaffer told me when I met him in New York later that evening, "These kids can be very oppositional, powerful kids who can take years off your happy life. But they aren't bipolar."

"So what are they?"

"Attention-deficit disorder," he said. "Often with an ADD kid you think: 'My God, they're just like a manic adult.' But they don't grow up manic. And manic adults weren't ADD when they were children. But they're being labelled bipolar.

"That's an enormous label that's going to stay with you for the rest of your life. You're being told you have a condition which is going to make you unreliable, prone to terrible depressions and suicide."

The Debate Is Not Going Away

The debate around childhood bipolar is not going away. In 2008, *The New York Times* published excerpts from an internal hospital document in which Biederman promised to "move forward the commercial goals of Johnson & Johnson", the firm that funds his hospital unit and sells the antipsychotic drug Risperdal. Biederman has denied the allegations of conflict of interest.

Frances has called for the diagnosis of childhood bipolar to be thrown out of the next edition of *DSM*, which is now being drawn up by the American Psychiatric Association.

This article shouldn't be read as a polemic against psychiatry. There are a lot of unhappy and damaged people out there whose symptoms manifest themselves in odd ways. I get irritated by critics who seem to think that because psychiatry has elements of irrationality, there is essentially no such thing as mental illness. There is. Childhood bipolar, however, seems to me an example of things having gone palpably wrong.

On the night of 13 December 2006, in Boston, Massachusetts, 4-year-old Rebecca Riley had a cold and couldn't sleep. Her mother, Carolyn Riley, gave her some cold medicine, and some of her bipolar medication, and told her she could sleep on the floor next to the bed. When she tried to wake Rebecca the next morning, she discovered her daughter was dead.

The autopsy revealed that Rebecca's parents had given her an overdose of the antipsychotic drugs she had been prescribed for her bipolar disorder. They had got into the habit of feeding her the medicines to shut her up when she was being annoying. They were both convicted of Rebecca's murder.

Rebecca had been diagnosed as bipolar at two-and-a-half, and given medication by an upstanding psychiatrist who was a fan of Biederman's research into childhood bipolar. Rebecca had scored high on the *DSM* checklist, even though like most toddlers she could barely string a sentence together.

Shortly before her trial, Carolyn Riley was interviewed on CBS's *60 Minutes* show by Katie Couric:

KC: Do you think Rebecca really had bipolar disorder?

CR: Probably not.

KC: What do you think was wrong with her now?

CR: I don't know. Maybe she was just hyper for her age.

Periodical and Internet Sources Bibliography

The following articles have been selected to supplement the diverse views presented in this chapter.

Melinda Beck	"ADHD: Why More Adults Are Being Diagnosed," *Wall Street Journal*, April 6, 2010.
Kiki Chang, Gabrielle Carlson, and Stephen M. Strakowski	"Is Bipolar Disorder Overdiagnosed in Children and Adolescents? A Virtual Debate," Medscape, September 10, 2010. www.medscape.com.
Daniel F. Connor	"Problems of Overdiagnosis and Overprescribing in ADHD," *Psychiatric Times*, August 11, 2011.
MacLean Gander	"Is ADHD Overdiagnosed?," *USA Today*, December 8, 2012.
Benjamin I. Goldstein	"Pediatric Bipolar Disorder: More than a Temper Problem," *Pediatrics*, June 1, 2010.
Stuart K. Kaplan	"Mommy, Am I Really Bipolar?," *Newsweek*, June 19, 2011.
Scott O. Lilienfeld and Hal Arkowitz	"Do Kids Get Bipolar Disorder?," *Scientific American*, July 3, 2012.
Stacy Notaras Murphy	"Underdiagnosed and Overwhelmed," *Counseling Today*, January 1, 2011.
Tara Parker-Pope	"Attention Disorders Can Take a Toll on Marriage," *New York Times*, July 20, 2010.
Jill Rubolino	"Autism Is Not Mental Illness: Get It Out of the DSM," *Age of Autism*, April 20, 2009.
Alan Zarembo	"Autism Boom: An Epidemic of Disease or of Discovery?," *Los Angeles Times*, December 11, 2011.

OPPOSING
VIEWPOINTS®
SERIES

CHAPTER 2

What Factors Contribute to Behavioral Disorders?

Chapter Preface

The cause or causes of obsessive-compulsive disorder (OCD) continue to elude researchers. At the height of popularity of psychoanalysis in the twentieth century, it was theorized that such obsessions and compulsions stemmed from unresolved conflicts hidden in the subconscious mind. "The symptoms of OCD symbolize the patient's unconscious struggle for control over drives that are unacceptable at a conscious level," says Wayne K. Goodman, chair of the Psychiatry Department at the Mount Sinai Medical Center in New York, of the theory. "Psychoanalysis offers an elaborate metaphor for the mind, but it is not grounded in evidence based on studies of the brain," he points out.

Still, some experts consider major life events to be factors in how the disorder takes shape or in its severity. In a study of two hundred patients conducted in 1988, 29 percent believed that a significant life event—and increased personal responsibilities, in particular—brought on their condition. For example, the death of a family member may give rise to persistent, irrational fears for the safety and lives of loved ones, and the resulting stress can exacerbate the symptoms. "Patients with OCD are likely to treat every action as if there is a lot at stake. Therefore, they check everything," states Frederic Neuman, director of the Anxiety and Phobia Center at White Plains Hospital in New York, adding, "They *start off* with the idea that the world is a threatening place."

Because it is considered a neurological disorder, current theories of what causes OCD focus on the human brain, specifically chemical imbalances in regions that control repetitive behaviors. Researchers have discovered an association between the illness and low levels of serotonin, a neurotransmitter that plays a role in the communication of nerve cells, and serotonin reuptake inhibitors (SRIs) are observed to be effective medications. But this treatment does not provide a clear-cut explanation, as it takes weeks before SRIs alleviate symptoms, according to Goodman. "The effectiveness of SRIs in OCD furnishes important clues about serotonin, but additional research is needed to identify the precise role of this neurochemical in the treatment and cause of OCD," he states.

The authors of the viewpoints in the following chapter debate the origins of and factors contributing to OCD and other behavioral disorders.

| *"By looking across the genomes of children with ADHD, [researchers] have uncovered direct evidence of a genetic contribution to the disorder."*

Attention-Deficit/Hyperactivity Disorder Has a Genetic Basis

Penny Bailey

Penny Bailey is a corporate writer at the Wellcome Trust, a charitable foundation based in London, England. In the following viewpoint, Bailey discusses the genetic link of attention-deficit/hyperactivity disorder (ADHD) with Anita Thapar, clinical academic child and adolescent psychiatrist at Cardiff University School of Medicine in Wales. Research has long supported that ADHD is hereditary, and a recent study found that a specific gene variant is associated with the antisocial behavior present in the disorder, claims Bailey. Furthermore, Thapar states that the genome, or set of chromosomes, in children with ADHD share a specific discrepancy and there is overlap between the regions associated with schizophrenia and autism. Understanding these genetic causes can help better tailor the treatment of ADHD in children and lessen its social stigma, Thapar maintains.

As you read, consider the following questions:

1. How is ADHD widely perceived, according to Bailey?

2. What did researchers discover about the genetic variant COMT, as described by the author?

3. What does Thapar, as quoted by Bailey, say is important about ADHD's showing overlap in the genome with autism and schizophrenia?

Attention deficit hyperactivity disorder (ADHD) is a common mental health problem that severely disrupts people's lives. . . . "We know very little about what causes ADHD and how it develops," says Professor Anita Thapar, Clinical Academic Child and Adolescent Psychiatrist at Cardiff University School of Medicine. Indeed, children with ADHD are not always taken seriously, or given public sympathy. ADHD is often seen as an excuse for bad behaviour and laziness, or simply blamed on bad parenting, For many, it is not a 'serious' disorder, even though it affects one to two per cent of children, and is one of the most common reasons for children to use mental health services.

"One of the things I'm really struck by when I see families and children in the clinic is this issue about public perceptions of ADHD, and the media representations of ADHD," says Professor Thapar. "My sincere hope is that, through these scientific findings, the general public and services will take ADHD seriously."

Over the last 15 years, Professor Thapar and colleagues have been building evidence to show that ADHD has genetic links. Now, by looking across the genomes of children with ADHD, they have uncovered direct evidence of a genetic contribution to the disorder as well as intriguing links to autism and schizophrenia.

Genetic Clues

ADHD's hallmark symptoms are hyperactivity, inattention and impulsiveness: children are restless and fidget, can't concentrate on schoolwork or TV, and are very impulsive, not waiting their turn, and doing things without thinking. Most children show at least some of these symptoms at times in their development, but for those with ADHD, the symptoms are not only extremely severe, but they are also inappropriate for the age of the child and are present in more than one setting.

The problems accompanying ADHD disrupt both learning at school and relationships with family and friends in childhood. Adults with ADHD are more likely to have difficulties getting or keeping employment, abuse drugs and alcohol, and end up in prison or with a criminal record.

So what do researchers currently understand about the genetic basis of the ADHD?

"We've known for many years that ADHD tends to run in families, so there is likely to be a genetic contribution," says Professor Thapar. "Over a decade ago, we studied identical and non-identical pairs of twins, and showed that ADHD is indeed highly heritable, as people who have close relatives with ADHD are more likely to develop it themselves."

Another clue came from a study of 'candidate genes' between 2000 and 2003, funded by the Wellcome Trust. This study looked at a selection of genes affecting the brain and behaviour in 300 children with ADHD from clinics in England and Wales. They found that a variant in a gene called COMT, which is involved in the breakdown of the brain transmitter dopamine, was linked to antisocial behaviour in those with ADHD.

Furthermore, the children with ADHD were more likely to have a variant that produced a more active version of the

Blinded to the Biological Facts

Sensationalist authors make broad claims that a certain lifestyle intervention will "cure" ADHD, suggesting that our modern culture is perhaps the cause. Or that like fragile flowers, children with ADHD blossom only when raised "well"—whatever that means. Yet there are endless numbers of well-meaning, hard-working parents raising children who battle problems with focus, impulsivity, hyperactivity, and all the related disruptions ADHD triggers—and it has nothing to do with anything that happened or failed to happen at home. Because of these baseless societal claims, parents often end up blaming themselves: *If only I could come up with a new plan, or figure out how to motivate my child, ADHD would go away.* Through no fault of their own, parents often become blinded to the straightforward biological facts.

Mark Bertin, The Family ADHD Solution, *2011.*

COMT enzyme that breaks down dopamine faster in the brain—a finding that has since been replicated by many other groups in different countries.

Searching Across the Genome

This was important progress, but complex disorders such as ADHD are likely to affect many different genes. In 2007, Professor Thapar and colleagues were awarded funding by the Wellcome Trust to investigate the genomes of children with ADHD, to find out which other regions might be involved in the disorder.

Findings in a paper published in the *Lancet* in September 2010 confirmed that there are differences in certain parts of the genome between children with and without ADHD. These discrepancies were in copy number variants (CNVs)—pieces of the genome that are duplicated, sometimes many times, or deleted altogether. "These children had double the rate of rare, large CNVs than normal controls," says Professor Thapar.

Another exciting finding was that the CNVs associated with ADHD occur in regions of the genome associated with both autism and schizophrenia. Although these are clinically separate conditions from ADHD—and the study specifically excluded people who might have them—there appears to be a genetic overlap.

"We've known that ADHD and autism share some clinical similarities," says Professor Thapar, "but they've always been regarded as separate conditions. Now that we've found that there is an overlap between regions of the genome that harbour CNVs related to ADHD, and regions implicated in autism and schizophrenia, it brings these neurodevelopmental disorders together. That is important because some people believe ADHD is better viewed as a behavioural problem or social construct rather than a neurodevelopmental disorder that shares biological similarities with autism and schizophrenia."

Also emerging from the study was the finding that the increased rate of CNVs in ADHD was not related to intellectual disability. "A proportion of people with ADHD do have intellectual or learning disabilities, so it could be that the CNVs we found are related to IQ, not to ADHD," she explains. "But we've shown that these CNVs are not just found in people with learning disabilities."

Understanding the Causes of ADHD

Professor Thapar hopes that this research will stimulate scientific interest in this area. "These aren't the sort of findings that will lead to a test for ADHD," she points out. "We already have that—the best method for diagnosis at present is to ask the right sorts of detailed, careful questions. But this type of research might help us to refine our diagnoses or define meaningful subgroups."

"Most importantly, the results can help us understand the causes and biology of ADHD, which can suggest how it might be treated. At the moment, we only have a limited range of treatments available; but if we can understand what is happening in the brain during the development of ADHD, we might be able to develop more precisely tailored, more effective treatments."

Equally important is the impact such findings can have for families, as parents are often blamed for their children's 'bad behaviour'. "The parents of children with ADHD that I meet in the clinic are heroes," says Professor Thapar. "And they don't get a break—they don't get any sympathy, as there's no visible problem with their child. The affected children struggle with school and rejection by their peers. Now we can show people that these children have a neurodevelopmental disorder with an observable genetic contribution."

"We've come a long way in the last 20 years in our understanding of autism and schizophrenia, such that people hopefully don't encounter the sorts of stigma that they might have in the past. I hope that this will help do the same for children and families with ADHD."

"*There is no contradiction at all between biological and sociological analyses of ADHD or any other condition referred to as a disorder.*"

Attention-Deficit/Hyperactivity Disorder Has a Sociological and Evolutionary Basis

Peter Gray

The rapid increase of attention-deficit/hyperactivity disorder (ADHD) is attributed to differences in brain structure, but, as Peter Gray contends in the following viewpoint, changes in education and the condition's evolutionary origins should be acknowledged as factors. He argues that increased competitiveness and standardized testing in schools correlate with the jump in ADHD diagnoses and that otherwise normal behaviors are now considered abnormal. Moreover, ADHD-like traits—such as distractibility, impatience, and difficulty following instructions—are socially valuable in the context of natural selection and evolution, Gray asserts. And while studies of brain differences in individuals with ADHD offer insight into the condition, Gray insists that they have no relevance to whether the condition is a disor-

*der or a normal variation of personality. Gray is a research pro-
fessor in psychology at Boston College and author of* Free to
Learn *and* Psychology, *a textbook.*

As you read, consider the following questions:

1. In what three ways is the diagnosis of ADHD related to
   schooling, according to Gray?

2. How is distractibility socially valuable, according to the
   author?

3. How does Gray view the research suggesting that people
   with ADHD have differences in the prefrontal cortex
   and fewer dopamine receptors?

Last month [July 2010] I posted an essay linking the dramatic increase in diagnosed ADHD (Attention Deficit Hyperactivity Disorder) to our increasingly restrictive system of
schooling. I presented evidence there that (a) the official
DSM-IV [*Diagnostic and Statistical Manual of Mental Disorders*, 4th ed.] diagnostic criteria for ADHD focus primarily on
school-related issues such as sitting in seat, completing assignments, and not interrupting teachers; (b) most diagnoses of
ADHD begin with referrals from teachers or other school personnel; (c) teachers' ratings, if used alone, would produce far
more ADHD diagnoses than is the case when those ratings are
balanced by parents' ratings; and (d) the rapid increase in
ADHD diagnoses occurred over the same period that high-
stakes standardized testing increasingly dominated the school
environment. My overriding point was that, because of the increased competitive and standardized nature of schooling, behaviors that in the past would have been regarded as within
the range of normal are now considered to be abnormal. At
present, in the United States, roughly 12% of boys and 4% of
girls have been diagnosed with ADHD. What kind of a society

are we if we consider 12% of boys (*one out of every eight*) to be *mentally disordered* in this way and in need of strong psychoactive drugs as treatment?

Some people who commented on that post objected to my sociological analysis by referring to evidence that the brains of people diagnosed with ADHD are in some ways different from those of other people. To them, the evidence of a brain difference is somehow proof that ADHD is a "medical" or "biological" disorder and that a sociological analysis of it is out of place. But if you give it some thought, you will quickly realize that there is no contradiction at all between biological and sociological analyses of ADHD or any other condition referred to as a disorder. My goal in that essay was to explain the extraordinary increase in rate of ADHD diagnosis that has occurred over the last two or three decades. I don't think that increase is primarily due to a change in brain structures in the general population; I think it is primarily due to a change in social values and especially in the conditions of schooling. Today, as a society, we are far less tolerant of children who don't adapt well to our system of compulsory education than we were in the past, and so we diagnose them and give them drugs.

For a somewhat (but not fully) analogous case, consider homosexuality. Homosexuality is biologically a condition of the brain; but the decision to label it as a disorder, or not a disorder, is a social judgment. Until 1973, homosexuality was on the American Psychiatric Association's list of official mental disorders, but in that year it was removed. Suddenly, gay people were no longer "disordered." That decision clearly reflected a change in social values, a change that made it possible for people with the brain condition of homosexuality to live happier lives than they had been able to before, when they more or less had to stay in the closet and were subject to terrible abuse and even arrest if they did not. With regard to homosexuality we have as a society become more liberal and accepting. With regard to the kind of childhood rambunctious-ness and impulsiveness that leads to a diagnosis of ADHD, however, we have as a society become less liberal and accept-ing.

The story for ADHD, of course, is not fully analogous to that for homosexuality. The condition we call ADHD is clearly one that can vary in degree. A few people—and I think that is *very* few people—who are diagnosed with ADHD have the condition to such an extreme degree that most of us would consider it to be a disorder, worthy of some kind of treat-ment, under almost any social conditions. But most people with the diagnosis have the condition to a much lesser degree than that—a degree that interferes especially with schooling and certain other school-like activities, as they are structured today, but may actually be helpful in other settings. . . .

Impulsiveness Is Basic to ADHD

According to the most widely accepted cognitive model of it, the fundamental problem in ADHD is not one of attention so much as one of impulsiveness. By a wide variety of measures, people diagnosed with ADHD are more impulsive, less reflec-tive and controlled, than other people. This impulsiveness is believed to underlie all or most of the distinguishing behav-ioral characteristics shown by such people. Impulsiveness leads them to be *easily distractible*, which is why they are seen as *inattentive*. It also leads them to be *impatient* and *restless*, unable to tolerate tedium or to sit still unless something truly grabs and retains their interest, which is why they may be seen as *hyperactive*. And it leads them to be highly *emotionally reac-tive*; they tend to respond immediately, emotionally, overtly, to stressful or otherwise arousing situations. The model is no doubt overly simplistic, but it is nevertheless useful as a be-ginning point for thinking and talking about ADHD.

Cognitive psychologists and neuroscientists commonly use the term *executive control* to label the mechanisms by which

Expecting Children to Self-Regulate

Whatever one's views as to whether ADHD-type behaviour could be adaptive or not, it is only relatively recently in our history that we have been required to be self-regulating, problem-solving, forward-planning individuals. In the past, when children were required to behave in this way—for example, being expected to sit still and behave in church—there would have been rigid social expectations and sanctions to ensure compliance. This is not so in today's world. Today's adults expect children to be *wholly* self-regulating in a society that has become almost devoid of social structure of any kind.

Angela Southall, The Other Side of ADHD, *2007.*

the brain inhibits impulsive behavior, reflects, and then acts on the basis of reflection rather than impulse. Although executive control is generally thought of as a good thing, it seems obvious that it can also, if too strong, be a bad thing. The opposite of impulsive is inhibited. Some people are too inhibited for their own good. They stew constantly over what is the right thing to do, or over the possible negative consequences of every alternative, and therefore they don't do anything. While the highly controlled person sits and watches an emergency, trying to figure out the best possible response and worrying about the risks, the impulsive person jumps in and saves someone's life.

Humans Are a Highly Social Species

Most psychologists would say that psychological well-being is maximized by a certain optimal degree of executive control. The overly controlled person suffers from too much inhibition, and the overly impulsive person suffers from too little of it. I agree with that when we are talking about extremes. However, between the extremes there is a broad range on the control-impulsiveness dimension that is potentially quite compatible with psychological well-being and contribution to society. The trick, for each person, is to find niches within their environment that play to their strengths rather than to their weaknesses. In general, people who are highly controlled are great in jobs that require lots of reflection and relatively little action, and people who are highly impulsive are great in jobs that require lots of action with relatively little time for reflection. This has nothing to do with degree of intelligence. You can be intelligent and impulsive, making terrific snap judgments; and you can also be intelligent and reflective, making good judgments after thinking things through very carefully.

We are a highly social species. Never in our evolution as humans did we survive on our own, as separate individuals. We always depended on our cooperative relationships with others, and the same is true today. From this point of view, it is not surprising that natural selection would have supported a broad range of personality types. People of different personalities are well adapted to make different kinds of contributions to the community (and, thereby, also to themselves). Ideally, they would all be valued for the unique contributions they can make and would be helped by others in their areas of weakness. Certainly this was true in hunter-gatherer bands, and we see it operating today within healthy families, tight-knit friendship groups, and well-run businesses. The dimension of control versus impulsivity is, I suggest, one of the most obvious and important dimensions of normal, healthy personality variation. In the course of our evolution, it was valuable that some of us were relatively more controlled and reflective while others of us were relatively less controlled and more action-oriented than the majority.

It is not hard at all to think of conditions in which ADHD-like characteristics are socially valuable. *Distractibility* may result in efficient monitoring of changes in the environment, so that sudden dangers or new opportunities, which others would have missed, are detected. *Impatience* may be a valuable counterweight to the tendency to dwell too long on a way of thinking or behaving that isn't going anywhere. *Impulsive action* may underlie bravery in the face of dangers that would keep others immobile. *Difficulty following instructions* may imply independence of mind, which can lead to novel ways of seeing and doing things. *Emotional reactivity* may be a good counterweight to the tendency of overly controlled people to hold in their emotions and ruminate. One thing I have observed (informally) in people diagnosed with ADHD is that they rarely hold grudges; they let their emotions out and then get over it.

But in school, of course, all of these things are bad; they all get you into trouble. School—at least school as usually defined these days—is a place where you must concentrate on what you are told to concentrate on, no matter how tedious; follow the teachers' directions, no matter how inane; complete assignments for the sheer purpose of completing them, even though they accomplish nothing useful; and, while doing all of that, control your emotions. The school classroom is not a place that values bravery, inventiveness, independence of mind, or emotional reactivity. So, of course, impulsiveness comes across as a "disorder" in school. Today we tend to define school as the primary environment of the child, so impulsiveness is the number one mental disorder of childhood.

Brain Function in ADHD

Neuroscientists have made much-touted progress in understanding the brain, but still that understanding is extremely superficial. We have no idea, really, how the brain does any of the amazing things it does (beyond the simplest reflexes), but we do have some ideas about which parts of the brain are most involved in which functions. The areas of the brain that seem to be most crucial for executive control appear to lie within the prefrontal lobes of the cerebral cortex and in connections between the prefrontal cortex and other parts of the brain (including the striatum and the basal ganglia), which are involved in initiating and inhibiting actions. At least some of these neural connections involve dopamine as the predominant neurotransmitter, which is significant because the stimulant drugs used most often to treat ADHD—preparations of amphetamine or methylphenidate—all exert their effects by prolonging the action of dopamine in neural synapses.

Not surprisingly, therefore, researchers looking for brain correlates of ADHD have focused on the prefrontal cortex and on dopamine. The results of such research are highly variable from lab to lab, with much controversy resulting. Also, the results are often confounded because most of the people in the ADHD groups have been treated with stimulant drugs, either at the time of study or in the past, so it is not clear if any brain difference observed is a correlate of the ADHD itself or is caused by long-term effects of the drug. However, overall, the research suggests that people with ADHD, compared to other people, may have (a) slightly reduced neural mass in the prefrontal cortex, (b) reduced activity in some parts of the prefrontal cortex while performing certain tests of executive function; and (c) fewer dopamine receptors in certain parts of the brain that receive input from the prefrontal cortex. All of these differences are highly variable from individual to individual and observable only as a result of statistical averaging. So far no biological marker of ADHD has been found that is sufficiently reliable to be used as an aid in diagnosis.

The studies of brain differences are interesting, but they have no bearing at all on the question of whether ADHD is a disorder or a normal personality variation. All personality variations have a basis in the brain. Of course they do. The brain controls all of behavior, so any difference that is reflected in behavior must exist in the brain. The only means by which natural selection can produce personality variation is through altering genes that affect the brain. If people diagnosed with ADHD differ behaviorally in any consistent way from other people, then their brains must in some way be different. Even if the research to date showed no difference at all in the brains of people with and without an ADHD diagnosis, I would argue that a difference exists. The researchers just haven't looked in the right places, or with the right tools or systems of measurement.

> *"The evidence linking vaccines and autism continues to mount."*

Vaccines Cause Autism

Michael Snyder

In the following viewpoint, Michael Snyder argues that although the pharmaceutical industry disputes it, autism is linked to childhood vaccinations. A growing body of evidence demonstrates that otherwise healthy toddlers sicken, stop talking, and show the signs of autism shortly after intensive vaccination protocols, he claims, coinciding with the disorder's epidemic in the United States. Snyder also warns that mercury-containing thimerosal, a preservative used in vaccines, causes brain and neurological damage. Nonetheless, parents who decline to have their children vaccinated, he asserts, are subjected to harsh consequences.

Michael Snyder is an attorney and writer. He blogs at The American Dream, *offering commentary on issues facing the United States.*

As you read, consider the following questions:

1. In the author's opinion, why will the mainstream media not admit that a link between vaccinations and autism exists?

2. According to Snyder, what does the Environmental Protection Agency state about the effects of methylmercury on a baby's growing brain?

3. What examples does the author offer as the consequences that parents suffer for not vaccinating their children?

According to the Centers for Disease Control and Prevention [CDC], the number of children in the United States with autism has risen by 78 percent over the past decade. It is now estimated that 1 out of every 88 children in the United States has some form of autism disorder. Our schools are absolutely packed with "special needs" children and millions of parents are desperately trying to figure out why so many kids are having such severe developmental problems. Strangely, most autistic children start out perfectly normal. Most of them develop just fine for the first year or two and then something dramatic happens. So what could that possibly be? Well, there is a secret that you are not supposed to know. That secret is that vaccines are one of the primary causes of autism. As the number of vaccines being administered to our children has risen, so has the percentage of our children with autism. Today, in some areas of the United States more than 30 vaccines are being given to young children before the age of 3. When you inject so much mercury and so much other toxic material directly into the bloodstreams of vulnerable young children, bad stuff is bound to happen. The evidence linking vaccines and autism continues to mount, and yet the pharmaceutical establishment continues to vigorously deny that there could possibly be any link between the two.

Each year, there are thousands upon thousands of parents that take their perfectly healthy toddlers into the doctor to get a vaccine and later end up deeply regretting it. Shortly after taking one too many vaccines, many children get sick, stop talking and never recover. The parents of those children are left absolutely devastated.

If you start surfing around the Internet, you can find enough testimonies like this to keep you reading for days on end.

But for the pharmaceutical establishment, a link must never be admitted between vaccines and autism. Hundreds of billions of dollars of profits are at stake, and the legal implications of admitting that vaccines cause autism would be absolutely mind blowing.

The big pharmaceutical companies will never, ever, ever, ever admit a link. And since those companies also spend billions of dollars advertising on the mainstream media, the mainstream media will never admit a link either.

It is all about the money.

So they have to act incredibly puzzled about what is causing cases of autism to dramatically surge in the United States.

And "dramatically surge" is actually an understatement.

The Epidemic Is Hard to Deny

It is getting really hard to deny that the epidemic of autism in America is absolutely exploding. The following is from a recent CNN article:

> In 2000 and 2002, the autism estimate was about 1 in 150 children. Two years later 1 in 125 8-year-olds had autism. In 2006, the number was 1 in 110, and the newest data—from 2008—suggests 1 in 88 children have autism.

So what is causing this?

The mainstream media is floating all kinds of bizarre theories.

But an increasing number of U.S. parents are coming to one conclusion. Despite overwhelming propaganda in the mainstream media that vaccines do not cause autism, one poll found that one out of every four parents now believe that vaccines cause autism.

So why are so many parents not listening to the "experts"?

Well, it is because of what they have seen in real life. The following is from a recent *Huffington Post* article:

It's a fact that many children with ASD [autism spectrum disorder] regressed following normal development just as they were receiving multiple vaccines at regular doctor visits. Health officials say the timing is entirely coincidental.

Regression usually occurs between 12 and 24 months, though one study found that some children show signs of autism as early as six months, but never before that age.

By six months of age, most U.S. children have received about 18 inoculations containing 24 vaccines against nine diseases. Over the next two years or so, they will receive another nine shots containing 14 vaccines against 12 diseases.

So whether a child regresses at six months, or 18 months, the tragedy happens during a period of intensive vaccination. In many cases, parents report that the child had an abnormal reaction after being vaccinated (seizures, spiking fevers, diarrhea, lethargy, high-pitched screaming and/or other symptoms).

If your kid stopped talking within days (or even hours) after receiving a vaccine, how would you feel?

The big pharmaceutical companies have funded many studies to try to show that there is no link between vaccines and autism, but many independent studies contradict the findings of those corporate-funded studies. The following is from an article by [writer and conspiracy theorist] Paul Joseph Watson:

Epidemiologist Tom Verstraeten and Dr. Richard Johnston, an immunologist and pediatrician from the University of Colorado, both concluded that thimerosal was responsible for the dramatic rise in cases of autism but their findings were dismissed by the CDC.

Cases of autism in the U.S. have now increased by over 2,700 per cent since 1991, which is when vaccines for children doubled, and the number of immunizations is only increasing. Just one in 2,500 children were diagnosed with autism before 1991, whereas one in 91 children now have the disease, up from one in 150 just six years ago.

Pumping Mercury into Children

So what is so bad about thimerosal?

Well, thimerosal contains mercury, which is one of the most toxic substances known to mankind. Mercury has been proven to severely impair neurological development. The following comes directly from the EPA [Environmental Protection Agency] website:

> For fetuses, infants, and children, the primary health effect of methylmercury is impaired neurological development. Methylmercury exposure in the womb, which can result from a mother's consumption of fish and shellfish that contain methylmercury, can adversely affect a baby's growing brain and nervous system. Impacts on cognitive thinking, memory, attention, language, and fine motor and visual spatial skills have been seen in children exposed to methylmercury in the womb.

So why in the world would we want to pump massive amounts of mercury into our young children when their brains are just starting to develop?

It is literally insane to do this!

Many other countries around the world have recognized this and have banned thimerosal from vaccines.

The following comes from an article by [health writer] Dawn Prate:

> In 1977, a Russian study found that adults exposed to ethylmercury, the form of mercury in thimerosal, suffered brain damage years later. Studies on thimerosal poisoning also de-

scribe tubular necrosis and nervous system injury, including obtundation, coma and death. As a result of these findings, Russia banned thimerosal from children's vaccines in 1980. Denmark, Austria, Japan, Great Britain and all the Scandinavian countries have also banned the preservative.

So why is it not banned in the United States?

And why do so many American parents still allow it to be pumped at very high levels directly into the bloodstreams of their precious young children?

There are thousands upon thousands of parents that are willing to testify that they would never have allowed their children to be vaccinated if they could go back and do it again. . . .

Not Just Children Are Being Harmed

But it isn't just young children that are being harmed by vaccines.

Thousands upon thousands of pregnant women have lost their babies very shortly after taking vaccines.

Thousands upon thousands of adults have become permanently disabled very shortly after taking vaccines. . . .

The good news is that if your child has autism there is hope.

Once you understand that vaccines can cause autism, it becomes much easier to treat it. The following is a quote from Dr. Russell Blaylock:

> Studies of autistic children have frequently shown very high levels of mercury, with no other source but vaccines found for the exposure. These levels are equal to those seen in adults during toxic industrial exposures. Several autism clinics have found dramatic improvements in the behavior and social interactions in children from whom the mercury was chelated. Results depended on how soon the mercury was removed following exposure, but permanent damage can be caused if the metal is not chelated soon enough. Still, even

in cases of severe damage, because of the infant brain's tremendous reparative ability, improvements are possible. The problem of autism involves numerous body systems including the gastrointestinal, immune and nervous systems; as a result we see numerous infections and magnified effects of malnutrition. Intrepid workers in the shadows, that is outside the medical establishment, have worked many miracles with these children using a multidisciplinary scientific approach completely ignored by the orthodoxy. Some children have even experienced a return to complete physiological normalcy.

So if your child has autism, do not give up hope.

There are things that can be done.

Sadly, authorities all over the nation are responding to the anti-vaccine movement by becoming harsher than ever with parents.

For example, all over America children that have not received all of the "required vaccines" are being banned from school.

In some instances, children are actually being taken away from their parents for not giving them the "proper" vaccines. In one recent case in Pennsylvania, a social worker took custody of a baby just after it had been born just because the mother would not consent to have the child vaccinated.

Complete and Utter Madness

This is complete and utter madness.

Shouldn't parents have the right to determine whether or not their young children will be pumped full of mercury and other toxic substances?

Shouldn't parents have the right to question whether it is a good idea to inject kids with dozens of vaccines before the age of 3?

But that is not the way that our system works. The big pharmaceutical companies fund the campaigns of our politicians, and then they get our politicians to bully us into taking their vaccines. . . .

There is so much that could be written about this subject, but hopefully this article will get you started.

The key is to do your own research. Don't blindly listen to the pharmaceutical companies or to anyone else.

Before you ever decide to vaccinate a child, educate yourself about vaccines as much as possible.

Once again this year, thousands upon thousands of American children will become permanently disabled needlessly.

How bad will autism have to get in America before we all finally admit the truth?

> *"The vaccine-autism scare has under-
> mined one of the greatest successes of
> preventive medicine."*

Anatomy of a Scare

Sharon Begley

*In the following viewpoint, Sharon Begley refutes the claim that
childhood vaccinations are a cause of autism. Begley says that a
1998 study hinting that the vaccine for measles, mumps, and rubella (MMR) triggered autism in children sparked a panic spread
by the press and policy makers, which was followed by a publi-
cized association of thimerosal, a vaccine preservative, to the disorder. The study has been retracted by the majority of its authors, and scientific evidence has mounted against the link
between vaccinations and autism, she maintains. But the antivaccine campaign led by lawyers, activists, and public figures
continues, Begley asserts, distracting attention and resources
from research into the actual causes of the disorder and treatments. Sharon Begley is the senior health and science correspon-
dent for Reuters news service and former science editor and col-
umnist at* Newsweek.

As you read, consider the following questions:

1. What happened in the backlash against vaccines after
   the 1998 study, as described by Begley?

Sharon Begley, "Anatomy of a Scare," *Newsweek*, vol. 153, no. 9, March 2, 2009. Copyright © 2009 by Newsweek. All rights reserved. Reproduced by permission.

2. As told by the author, what did an investigation reveal about the 1998 study?

3. What evidence does Begley cite to back her position that MMR vaccine is not linked to autism?

Like many people in London on that bleak February day in 1998, biochemist Nicholas Chadwick was eager to hear what the scientists would say. The Royal Free Hospital, where he was a graduate student in the lab of gastroenterologist Andrew Wakefield, had called a press conference to unveil the results of a new study. With flashbulbs popping, Wakefield stepped up to the bank of microphones: he and his colleagues, he said, had discovered a new syndrome that they believed was triggered by the MMR (measles, mumps, rubella) vaccine. In eight of the 12 children in their study, being published that day in the respected journal *The Lancet*, they had found severe intestinal inflammation, with the symptoms striking six days, on average, after the children received the MMR. But hospitals don't hold elaborate press conferences for studies of gut problems. The reason for all the hoopla was that nine of the children in the study also had autism, and the tragic disease had seized them between one and 14 days after their MMR jab. The vaccine, Wakefield suggested, had damaged the intestine—in particular, the measles part had caused serious inflammation—allowing harmful proteins to leak from the gut into the bloodstream and from there to the brain, where they damaged neurons in a way that triggered autism. Although in their paper the scientists noted that "we did not prove an association" between the MMR and autism, Wakefield was adamant. "It's a moral issue for me," he said, "and I can't support the continued use of [the MMR] until this issue has been resolved."

That's strange, thought Chadwick. For months he had been extracting genetic material from children's gut biopsies, looking for evidence of measles from the MMR. That was the crucial first link in the chain of argument connecting the MMR to autism: the measles virus infects the gut, causing inflammation and leakage, then gut leakage lets neurotoxic compounds into the blood and brain. Yet Chadwick kept coming up empty-handed. "There were a few cases of false positives, [but] essentially all the samples tested were negative," he later told a judicial hearing. When he explained the negative results, he told *Newsweek*, Wakefield "tended to shrug his shoulders. Even in lab meetings he would only talk about data that supported his hypothesis. Once he had his theory, he stuck to it no matter what." Chadwick was more disappointed than upset, figuring little would come from the *Lancet* study. "Not many people thought [Wakefield] would be taken that seriously," Chadwick recalls. "We thought most people would see the *Lancet* paper for what it was—a very preliminary collection of [only 12] case reports. How wrong we were."

The next day, headlines in the British press screamed, DOCTORS LINK AUTISM TO MMR VACCINE and BAN THREE-IN-ONE JAB, URGE DOCTORS AFTER NEW FEARS. That was mild compared with what followed. Hysteria over childhood vaccinations built to such a crescendo that Wakefield's nuanced warning—that it was specifically the triple vaccine, not single-disease vaccines (even measles), that posed a threat—was drowned out. In 2001, Prime Minister Tony Blair and his wife, Cherie, refused to say whether their son, then 19 months old, had received the MMR; rumors swirled that they had gone to France so the child could receive the measles vaccine alone. In 2003, a docudrama about Wakefield ran on British TV, depicting him as having his files stolen and his phone tapped by evil pharmaceutical companies intent on protecting their vaccines. As one reviewer described the show: "The MMR vaccine is coming to get our kids."

The MMR vaccine is the same on both sides of the Atlantic, so fears of childhood vaccines (of which U.S. health officials recommend 35 by age 6) started a backlash in the United

States, too, fueled in no small part by the fact that the incidence of autism was rising for reasons scientists could not fully explain. In California, for instance, the incidence of autism had risen from 6.2 per 10,000 births in 1990 to 42.5 in 2001. Groups of parents began refusing vaccines for their children. Within a few years of Wakefield's announcement, rates of MMR vaccinations in Britain fell from 92 percent to below 80 percent. Although there was no comparable nationwide decrease in the United States, pockets of resistance to vaccination appeared throughout the country, laying the groundwork for a sevenfold increase in measles outbreaks. Looking back from the perspective of 11 years, the panic seems both inevitable and inexplicable. Inevitable, because legitimate scientists publishing in respected journals produced evidence of a link between vaccines and autism, and because the press as well as politicians and even public-health officials stoked the mounting hysteria. Inexplicable because, by the early 2000s, scientific support for that link had evaporated as completely as the red dot on a baby's vaccinated thigh.

Scientists and government officials who defended the safety of childhood vaccines were not shy about attributing the fears to the science illiteracy of the public and the fearmongering of the press. In truth, however, after Wakefield's announcement there was a steady drumbeat of studies—not from kooks in basement labs but from real scientists working at real institutions and publishing in real, peer-reviewed journals—that backed him up. In 2002, pathologist John O'Leary of Coombe Women's Hospital in Dublin reported that he had found RNA from the measles virus in 7 percent of normal children—but in 82 percent of those with autism, suggesting that some children are unable to clear the vaccinated virus from their systems, resulting in autism. That same year, a Utah State University biologist reported finding high levels of antibodies against the measles virus in the blood and spinal fluid of autistic children; the MMR, he postulated, had triggered a hyperimmune response that attacked the children's brains. In 2003, gastroen-terologist Arthur Krigsman, then at New York University School of Medicine, reported finding what Wakefield had: that the guts of 40 autistic children were severely inflamed, lending support to the idea that leaks allowed pernicious compounds to make a beeline for the brain.

But these studies and others supporting the link between autism and the MMR were nothing compared with an ex-traordinary step that had been taken by the U.S. government and by one of the country's leading medical organizations. On July 7, 1999, the American Academy of Pediatrics (AAP) and the U.S. Public Health Service issued a warning about the pre-servative in many vaccines. Called thimerosal, it contains 49.6 percent ethylmercury by weight and had been used in vac-cines since the 1930s, including the diphtheria/tetanus/pertussis (DTP) and *Haemophilus influenzae* (Hib) vaccines (but not the MMR). The experts tried to be reassuring, saying in a statement there are "no data or evidence of any harm" from thimerosal. But, they continued, children's cumulative exposure to mercury from vaccines "exceeds one of the federal safety guidelines" for mercury. (By 2003, most childhood vac-cines did not contain thimerosal, though flu vaccines still did.) The AAP statement did not mention autism.

But on April 6, 2000, Rep. Dan Burton did. Burton had previously distinguished himself by his support for laetrile, the quack cancer remedy. Now he was chairing a congres-sional hearing on the link between vaccines and autism. His own grandson, Burton told an overflow audience filled with antivaccine activists, was perfectly normal until he received "nine shots on one day," after which he "quit speaking, ran around banging his head against the wall, screaming and hol-lering and waving his hands." Witnesses testified about their own tragedies, such as a child's "journey into silence" soon af-ter receiving the MMR vaccine. Wakefield, too, testified. Since his *Lancet* paper, he said, he had studied scores more children, identifying almost 150 in whom MMR had triggered autism. O'Leary, the Irish scientist who had confirmed Wakefield's finding of measles virus in the guts of children with autism, pronounced himself "here to say that Wakefield's hypothesis is correct." Now there were two explosive theories about the dangers of childhood vaccines: Wakefield's, that the MMR caused gut inflammation and the release of autism-causing proteins into the blood and brain, and the thimerosal theory, that the mercury in childhood vaccines damages the immune system and, possibly, the brain.

Burton's hearing was widely covered in the press, but the, attention was nothing compared with the flood of stories that were about to be unleashed. That November *60 Minutes* aired a segment featuring children who "appeared normal" until getting the MMR. On Nov. 10, 2002, the *New York Times Magazine* ran an article on "The Not-So-Crackpot Autism Theory," about thimerosal. It included news of an August 2002 study by the father-and-son team Mark and David Geier, who combed a federal database of reported "adverse events" after vaccinations. They found "increases in the incidence of autism" after children got thimerosal-containing vaccines compared with thimerosal-free vaccines. The following spring, the Geiers published another study: the more mercury in their vaccines, the more likely children were to develop autism.

By this time, mistrust of the scientific establishment—and of anyone defending vaccines—had mushroomed into something decidedly uglier. When pediatrician Paul Offit, a vaccine expert at the Children's Hospital of Philadelphia, testified before Burton's panel, he said that he had had his own children vaccinated, and gave their names. At a break, a congressional staffer pulled him aside and said, "Never, never mention the names of your own children in front of a group like this." The following year he received an e-mail threatening to "hang you by your neck until you are dead." The FBI deemed it credible and assigned him an armed guard during vaccine meetings at the U.S. Centers for Disease Control and Prevention.

The first cracks in the vaccine theories of autism appeared in early 2004. An investigation by British Journalist Brian Deer in *The Sunday Times* of London revealed that the children Wakefield described in the *Lancet* study had not simply arrived on the doorstep of the Royal Free. At least five were clients of an attorney who was working on a case against vaccine makers alleging that the MMR caused the children's autism. In addition, two years before the *Lancet* paper Wakefield had received £55,000 from Britain's Legal Aid Board, which supports research related to lawsuits. After meeting with Deer, *Lancet* editor Richard Horton told the British press, "If we knew then what we know now, we certainly would not have published the part of the paper that related to MMR . . . There were fatal conflicts of interest." On March 6, 10 of Wakefield's 12 coauthors formally retracted the paper's suggestion that the MMR and autism were linked.

Wakefield did not join them. Now executive director of a Texas nonprofit called Thoughtful House, which offers treatments for autism, he admits he was retained and paid by the lawyer for the parents of autistic children but denies that posed a conflict of interest. "At the time the children were referred to the Royal Free, none of the parents were involved in litigation, though some went on to do so," he says. The legal board's payment supported other vaccine-autism research he was conducting, Wakefield says, not that in the *Lancet* paper. "I will not be deterred from continuing to look after these children and research their problems," says Wakefield.

In 2005 Britain's General Medical Council, which licenses physicians, began a hearing in which Wakefield was charged with professional misconduct for, among other things, the alleged financial conflict of interest in the *Lancet* study. The investigation has since expanded, with new charges by journalist Deer that Wakefield or his coauthors misrepresented the

© raesidecartoon.com.

children's medical records. In particular, Deer reported that the children's gut and autism symptoms appeared long before their MMR rather than, as the 1998 *Lancet* study reported, right after. Wakefield denies doing anything improper, saying he "merely entered the documented findings into the *Lancet* paper."

The charges against Wakefield were the least of what was undermining the vaccine theory of autism. What would eventually become an overwhelming body of evidence showing that childhood vaccines did not increase the risk of autism began to pile up. In 2002 scientists led by Brent Taylor of the Royal Free reported that their study of 473 children had found no difference in the rates of autism between those who had received the MMR and those who had not, providing "further evidence against involvement of MMR vaccine in the initiation of autism," they wrote. Scientists in Finland, studying 2 million children, reached the same conclusion in a 2000 paper. So did scientists at Boston University, studying the medical records of 3 million children, in 2001. In 2004 a study of the medical records of 14,000 children in Britain found that the more thimerosal the children had been exposed to through vaccines, the less likely they were to have neurological problems. Also that year, the Institute of Medicine (IOM) in the United States, having reviewed 200-plus studies, rejected the vaccine-autism hypothesis. Not only did it find no evidence of a link—and, indeed, evidence against the existence of a link—but it took aim at the original 1998 *Lancet* paper by Wakefield's group. Because autism symptoms typically appear at the same age that children get the MMR, the panel said, it was inevitable that some children would first show symptoms of autism soon after being vaccinated. Coincidence is not causality.

If the IOM panel thought that would be the end of it, they were naive. From the halls of Congress to the airwaves to the pages of leading newspapers, true believers went at the vaccine-autism link more passionately than ever. After the IOM released its report, Rep. Dave Weldon of Florida, a physician, took to the House floor to denounce the CDC for its vaccine-autism research. The agency, Weldon charged, was guilty of "selective use of the data to make the associations [between vaccines and autism] disappear" and had engaged in "a public-relations campaign [on behalf of vaccines] rather than sound science."

The following year, a story by environmental lawyer Robert F. Kennedy Jr. called "Deadly Immunity" made the case against thimerosal in *Rolling Stone*. Activists used large chunks of the money they were raising from terrified parents to spread their message. On June 8, a full-page ad for Generation Rescue, which had been founded the month before to push the thimerosal theory, ran in the *New York Times*, proclaiming, "Mercury Poisoning and Autism: It Isn't a Coincidence." It included quotes from several politicians, with Burton stressing research that "indicated a direct link between exposure to mercury and autism," and Sen. John Kerry saying "mercury has been linked to autism." Later that year, a book titled "Evidence of Harm: Mercury in Vaccines and the Autism Epidemic," by journalist David Kirby, got huge attention in the media. Kirby appeared on [the popular talk radio show] "Imus in the Morning" several times, as did politicians supporting his thesis. Sen. Joseph Lieberman, citing the growing incidence of autism coupled with the increase in the number of required vaccines, said, "Make sure your kids are getting vaccines without thimerosal."

Throughout this saga, the "vaccines cause autism" side could claim more powerful persuaders than the dry-as-dust scientific papers and even drier scientists trying to reassure parents. On Sept. 18, 2007, model and actress Jenny McCarthy appeared on "The Oprah Winfrey Show" to promote her new book, "Louder Than Words," in which she describes curing her son Evan's autism—which she blames on the MMR—with diet and chelation, a process that chemically binds heavy compounds in the body so they can be excreted. Asked about the CDC statement that science does not link vaccines to autism, McCarthy said, "My science is Evan." Researchers were dumbfounded that so many parents rejected the conclusions of the CDC, the Institute of Medicine and the American Academy of Pediatrics (which after its thimerosal debacle had put itself foursquare behind childhood vaccines). "The issue for people like Jenny McCarthy isn't that doctors and scientists and public-health officials haven't listened to parents," writes Paul Offit in his 2008 book "Autism's False Prophets: Bad Science, Risky Medicine and the Search for a Cure." "It's that they've been unable to find any evidence to validate parents' concern."

The antivaccine campaign was having an effect. As parents postponed vaccinating their children, or refused vaccines entirely, children were suddenly catching preventable diseases, and some were dying. The number of measles cases in the United States reached 131 in 2008, the highest in decades. Last month [February 2009] five children in Minnesota became infected with Hib. Four developed serious complications; the fifth child died. Other parents, believing that yanking mercury out would cure a child's autism, opted for chelation. Unfortunately, it can pull out vital metals such as iron and calcium as well as toxic mercury and lead.

An overwhelming majority of vaccine and autism experts were convinced that parents were putting their children at real risk over a phantom fear. But perhaps no one understood that the MMR theory, in particular, was a house of cards better than molecular biologist Stephen Bustin of the University of London. In 2004 the U.K. High Court asked him to inspect the Dublin lab that had reported measles genes in the guts of autistic children right after they received the MMR, an important confirmation of Wakefield's theory. It was an uncomfortable situation, Bustin recalls, playing cop at another scientist's lab. But he discovered a number of problems. The genetic material the lab had found was DNA, but measles genes are made of RNA. The equipment was so poorly calibrated that its results depended on where in the machine the sample was placed. Wakefield defends his collaborator, saying that a later test confirmed "the fidelity and high quality of [the Dublin lab's] methods ... The original results that found measles virus genetic material in intestinal biopsies in 75 percent of the autistic children compared with 6 percent of the nonautistic controls still stand."

Under U.S. law, families who believe their child has been injured by a vaccine have their claims heard by a special "vaccine court." Since 1999 some 5,000 families had filed claims asserting that vaccines caused their child's autism. That is too many to try individually, so in 2004 they were combined into three test cases. One would represent the claim that MMR caused the children's autism, one that thimerosal in vaccines other than MMR did and one that the combination did. The last theory was tested with the case of Michelle Cedillo, a 12-year-old with severe autism; hearings began on June 11, 2007. Before it was over, the evidence would include 939 papers from journals and textbooks and testimony running thousands of pages. One of those testifying was Bustin, who explained that the finding of measles genes in autistic children rested on shoddy science. "Normally it hardly matters when a scientific paper gets it wrong," Bustin says. "But in this case, it matters a great deal."

On Feb. 12 Special Master George Hastings Jr. announced his decision in the Cedillo case. Every study conducted to test Wakefield's MMR hypothesis, he concluded, "found no evidence that the MMR vaccination is associated with autism." And the evidence "falls far short" of showing a thimerosal connection.

That is hardly the end of the legal cases. All three sets of parents in the test cases say they will take their claims against the manufacturers to civil court, hoping to convince juries—through the emotional power of tragically damaged children—of what they failed to prove to the vaccine court. And if those cases, too, absolve vaccines? In postings on antivaccine sites such as GenerationRescue.org and SafeMinds.org, parents have made clear that they think the system is rigged and that vaccines condemned their children to a lifetime of being barricaded behind the impregnable wall of autism. Perhaps it should not be a mystery why people refuse to believe science, with its tentative hypotheses, zigzag pathway to finding answers and a record of getting some things wrong before getting them right (see hormone-replacement therapy). On the day the court announced its decision, Offit pointed out that "tens of millions of dollars have been spent trying to answer these questions [about vaccines and autism]," but many people "refuse to believe the science." Perhaps, he mused, that's "because while it's very easy to scare people, it's very hard to unscare them."

And it's impossible to prove a negative such as "vaccines do not cause autism." The slim hope of finding a link—perhaps only children with specific genetic variants are at risk of developing autism as a result of vaccines; perhaps the vaccine is dangerous only in combination with other environmental triggers—keeps activists at the barricades. (They received some support in 2007, when the federal government settled the case of Hannah Poling, admitting that a vaccine had exacerbated a rare underlying cellular disorder and, as a result, brought on autistic symptoms.) Wakefield, unrepentant, slams the vaccine-court decision for "not being based on any definitive science." One powerful advocacy group, Autism Speaks, said after the decision that it will continue to support research into whether certain children with "underlying medical or genetic conditions may be more vulnerable to adverse effects of vaccines." Chief science officer Geraldine Dawson says they "owe it to the parents to listen and address their concerns. We don't want to close the door." Not even a door that, since it was opened 11 years ago this month, has let through such demons. It is bad enough that the vaccine-autism scare has undermined one of the greatest successes of preventive medicine and terrified many new parents. Most tragic of all, it has diverted attention and millions of dollars away from finding the true causes and treatments of a cruel disease.

> "A growing list of American warriors
> . . . have been diagnosed with PTSD
> and are struggling to readjust to civil-
> ian life."

Returning Soldiers Find Themselves in Fragile State

Christopher Curry

In the following viewpoint, Christopher Curry argues that the Iraq and Afghanistan wars have increased the prevalence of post-traumatic stress disorder (PTSD) among veterans. Unlike in previous wars, Curry emphasizes, multiple deployments are now the norm for soldiers, worsening the psychological impacts of combat. And recent studies found that PTSD affects up to 35 percent of returning veterans, who are also four times as likely to experience thoughts of suicide, he contends. Despite the Department of Veterans Affairs' increased attention to the trauma of war and to prevention programs, the author maintains, many veterans decline to seek help because they are trained to be self-reliant and show no vulnerability.

Christopher Curry is a city government reporter for Florida's Gainesville Sun.

As you read, consider the following questions:

1. As stated by the author, how much more likely are veterans of multiple deployments to suffer from PTSD?

2. According to Curry, what percent of returning Iraq and Afghanistan veterans complete the necessary treatment for PTSD?

3. Why is the estimated rate of suicide among veterans unclear, in the author's opinion?

From childhood, Marco Grosso dreamed of serving in the military. His family recalls him dressed in camouflage and playing army in the woods behind his family's home near Syracuse, N.Y.

In 2007, he graduated from high school and enrolled in the Marines, a fresh-faced 17-year-old aiming to fight for his country and become a military lifer.

Grosso served two tours in Afghanistan's brutal Helmand Province. There, in March 2010, as he rode in an armored vehicle, a land mine explosion knocked him unconscious and wrecked his life.

He returned to the battlefield three weeks later and was awarded a Purple Heart. It was only after he returned home and was diagnosed with a traumatic brain injury and Post Traumatic Stress Disorder [PTSD] that he learned the blast had cut short his military career.

He and three battle buddies, friends from his Camp LeJeune days [in North Carolina], moved to Gainesville [Florida] when they left the Marines. They were drawn here for school and work but mainly because they had experienced the college town's nightlife on several unauthorized jaunts from the North Carolina base and wanted another taste.

On Nov. 6, 2011, after a Sunday night out at a bar with his friends, Grosso returned to his Gainesville townhouse. Sometime after 11:30 p.m., he put on his Marine Corps dress blue uniform, put a rifle to his head and pulled the trigger.

He was 22 years old.

A note he left behind traced his despair to the land mine blast.

"I just want to say I love my family and friends very much and I'm sorry I had to do this," the note read in part. "I haven't been right in the head since I got blown up. I can't go threw (sic) this pathetic life anymore."

More than a year after surviving Afghanistan, Grosso had become a casualty of war.

He joined a growing list of American warriors who have been diagnosed with PTSD and are struggling to readjust to civilian life.

A National Concern

Veterans' struggles to reset their lives after witnessing the horrors of war have always been with us, said Jim Lynch, Alachua County's former longtime veterans services officer and a Vietnam veteran.

"It has been an issue dating back to the first war this country was ever involved in," Lynch said. "You cannot take a guy who is just out of school away from everyday life, put him in a war where he will see things that are absolutely horrendous, and expect him to come back afterward and be the same ordinary guy he was. It's just not going to happen. You're absolutely never the same person after you've seen a war."

In other eras, it was called shell shock or combat fatigue. What sets this generation's wars apart, experts say, are the repeated deployments to combat zones.

A 2010 study published in the *American Journal for Public Health* concluded [that] U.S. service members who had multiple deployments to combat zones were three times more likely to suffer from PTSD.

In the Iraq and Afghanistan wars, multiple deployments have been the norm, with the psychological impacts compounded.

PTSD rates are as high as 35 percent in returning veterans, and those veterans are four times as likely to have suicidal thoughts, according to three studies the *Journal of Traumatic Stress* published in 2009 and 2010.

One of the studies concluded that "significant barriers" remained for the treatment of PTSD and that fewer than 10 percent of the returning Iraq and Afghan veterans make it through the 10 to 12 weeks of treatment deemed necessary.

Suicide and Violence Follow Returning Vets

As veterans come home, accounts of PTSD-related incidences of suicide and violence also have followed.

In December [2011], an Army veteran of two tours in Iraq whose wife said he had PTSD was arrested after police said he doused his mother-in-law's Chiefland [Florida] house with gas, intent on setting it ablaze, and then shot and killed the family dog. His wife said he had been without his medications for more than six days.

As the wars in Iraq and Afghanistan have carried on over the past decade, the Department of Veterans Affairs has put more focus on the psychological trauma of war and programs such as its suicide prevention hotline.

At the same time, there remains no accurate count of how many returning veterans commit suicide or how the numbers for Iraq and Afghanistan compare with past wars, said Margaret C. Harrell with the Center for a New American Security, a Washington, D.C., think tank.

In 2010, the Department of Veterans Affairs estimated that 18 veterans commit suicide each day. But those numbers did not focus on specific wars and include data from only the 16 states that indicate veteran status in their reports to the Centers for Disease Control and Prevention's National Violent Death Index.

"We don't really know if things are worse than they used to be because we don't know how bad things are today," Harrell said. "We don't know how many veterans we are losing now, so we can't compare it to the past."

With large Veterans Administration medical complexes in Gainesville and Lake City, the North Florida/South Georgia Veterans Health System is the largest in the country in terms of employees and geographic area covered.

Kathleen Yacovelli, a clinical program manager focused on veterans returning from Iraq and Afghanistan, said an array of mental health, substance abuse and PTSD counseling services are available. Three full-time employees are focused solely on suicide prevention.

Vets Have Responsibility to Seek Help

Still, the responsibility remains on the veterans to seek help through these programs.

Grosso's family members said he had gone to a counselor but came away disillusioned. They said they also believed the government could have done more to assist him since his military records—paperwork they did not see until after his death—showed that significant mental health issues, including his distress about no longer being able to serve in the Marines, were known before his discharge.

They questioned if it was realistic to expect a young veteran with mental health issues and brain injury to reach out for help.

Anthony Surrett, a Desert Storm veteran and the commander of Gainesville's Veterans of Foreign Wars [VFW] Post 2811, said soldiers are trained to be tough, self-reliant and show no vulnerability.

It goes against that to reach out for help and open up about issues of suicidal thoughts and depression, said Surrett, who grew close to Grosso and his friends after they joined the post and were embraced by older generations of veterans.

"A young soldier who has seen his friends die in a combat zone, the last thing he is going to admit is he needs help," he said. "It has to be mandatory."

A Military Destiny

For Grosso, the military was a family tradition. His mother, Kathleen Hawker, is retired from the Army National Guard. His older brother Rocco Grosso, 24, serves in the U.S. Navy.

As a boy, Marco Grosso would sit for hours watching History Channel programs about World War I and World War II.

He wavered between enlisting in the Army or the Marines. When an Army recruiter missed an appointment at his home, Grosso considered that a sign of disrespect and joined the Marines.

At boot camp and at Camp LeJeune, he forged friendships with Josh Williams, 24, Andrew Winston, 24, and Patrick Lichenstein, 25. They would fight shoulder to shoulder in Afghanistan and later live together in Gainesville.

All of them came from families with deep traditions of military service. Each planned to make a career in the military. Each also knew that fighting a war on the other side of the world loomed.

"I joined for that reason—to go to war," Williams said. "I joined to go into the infantry."

The friends were deployed to Afghanistan in 2008. Winston described them as "very lucky" during that year's combat.

In early 2010, all but Lichenstein returned to the field. The fighting was far more heated, and convoys routinely hit improvised explosive devices [IEDs] and land mines. Williams sustained injuries in two IED attacks and was awarded two Purple Hearts.

Vets Find Return Home a Difficult Adjustment

A recent study focused on 199 military veterans who served in Iraq or Afghanistan after 2001 and who were referred to military behavioral health clinicians from primary care. Veterans who had depression or PTSD were five times as likely to report problems with family readjustment as those who did not, including feeling like guests in their own homes and reporting that their children acted afraid or without warmth toward them. Almost one-third of the veterans reported that their partners were afraid of them.

Committee on the Initial Assessment of Readjustment Needs of Military Personnel, Veterans, and their Families, Board on the Health of Selected Populations, Institute of Medicine, Returning Home from Iraq and Afghanistan: Preliminary Assessment of Readjustment Needs of Veterans, Service Members, and their Families, *2010.*

The land mine explosion that knocked Grosso unconscious also fractured several teeth and required stitches to his face. He recovered from the physical injuries and returned to the field.

In paperwork he later filed while applying for veterans benefits, Grosso described multiple grisly events that occurred after he returned to the field following the land mine blast that injured him, his mother said.

He recounted carrying body parts and bodies back from the site of an attack and he recalled an IED attack in which a close friend lost both legs.

In late 2010, Grosso left the Marines after he learned he would not be allowed to reenlist because of his PTSD. By last spring, all four friends were out of the Marines.

Band of Brothers

From late 2010 to the summer of 2011, the four friends moved to Gainesville and reunited. They enrolled in college or looked for work and enjoyed the good times a college town had to offer.

Lichenstein recalled how, before the arrival of his other friends, he struggled with PTSD issues of his own and—at one point—found himself without work or a place to live. Before Grosso even made it down to Gainesville, he rented a townhouse and told his friend to move in immediately and "hold down the fort."

"Marco came to the rescue," Lichenstein said. "It was just like being in the Marine Corps again. We just had that bond again if not stronger. It's easy being friends with someone you know will give their life for you."

Usually, Grosso was the outgoing, fun-loving, generous joker they first met, his friends said. He got a job with Brink's riding on another armored vehicle. Looking for the camaraderie of the military, Grosso persuaded his friends to join the local VFW post.

Surrett, who had a son close to Grosso's age serving in the Army in Afghanistan, recalled how he and Grosso would spend long afternoons at the post talking about the war and about Afghanistan over fried bologna sandwiches.

Grosso also volunteered to work with the children in the post's Milton Lewis Young Marines youth outreach program, where he loved to put the kids through grueling physical fitness training.

But there also were bouts with depression, struggles with memory loss and multiple prescriptions for antidepressants, friends and family said.

Most of the time, they said, he hid his inner struggles well, using a facade of happiness and humor.

"He was a lifer," Lichenstein said. "He missed the Marine Corps when he was out. He missed the bond. When you get out and you make civilian friends, they haven't been through the hell you have been through. The bond is not the same."

Thwarting a Suicide Attempt

The police report on Grosso's suicide included Williams' account of a night several weeks earlier.

After returning from a night out, Grosso stayed home while Williams and other friends went to the store. Williams received a phone call from Grosso, who was crying and speaking of suicide. Williams returned to the apartment, forced his way into Grosso's bedroom and had to wrestle a rifle away from him.

Williams stayed to keep watch over Grosso the rest of the night.

Then, less than a week before Veterans Day, Grosso took his own life.

Grosso's three friends remain in Gainesville—taking classes or working—and still stopping by the VFW post from time to time.

When they think of Grosso, they say they try to remember the good times—his generosity and propensity for off-color humor.

Grosso's mother said her son died before he received his first veterans check.

Last month [February 2012], she said she received a letter from President Barack Obama thanking her for her son's service to his country.

*"Anyone who fights in a war is changed
by it, but few are irreparably damaged."*

PTSD's Diagnostic Trap

Sally Satel

*Sally Satel is a resident scholar at the American Enterprise Insti-
tute for Public Policy Research (AEI). In the following viewpoint,
she claims that difficulty in readjusting after combat is often labeled as mental illness and abnormal distress, resulting in the
overdiagnosis of Iraq and Afghanistan war veterans with post-
traumatic stress disorder (PTSD). Satel points out that a new
rule enacted by the Veterans Administration qualifies veterans
for PTSD disability even if they did not experience the ordeal
firsthand. Also, injured soldiers can apply for and receive such
benefits without psychiatric treatment, the author continues.
Consequently, Satel argues that many young veterans are permitted to surrender to the trauma of war before pursuing recovery, which encourages them to assume a "sick role" and become
institutionally dependent.*

As you read, consider the following questions:

1. What does Satel question about gauging the mental injury resulting from war?

2. According to Satel, what did the assessment by Columbia University of a landmark Vietnam veterans and PTSD study find?

3. What would the author like to see happen with the diagnosis of PTSD in veterans?

Military history is rich with tales of warriors who return from battle with the horrors of war still raging in their heads. One of the earliest examples was enshrined by Herodotus, who wrote of an Athenian warrior struck blind "without blow of sword or dart" when a soldier standing next to him was killed. The classic term—"shell shock"—dates to World War I; "battle fatigue," "combat exhaustion," and "war stress" were used in World War II.

Modern psychiatry calls these invisible wounds posttraumatic stress disorder (PTSD). And along with this diagnosis, which became widely known in the wake of the Vietnam War, has come a new sensitivity—among the public, the military, and mental health professionals—to the causes and consequences of being afflicted. The Department of Veterans Affairs is particularly attuned to the psychic welfare of the men and women who are returning from Operation Iraqi Freedom and Operation Enduring Freedom. Last July, retired Army General Eric K. Shinseki, secretary of Veterans Affairs, unveiled new procedures that make it easier for veterans who believe they are disabled by wartime stress to file benefit claims and receive compensation. "[Psychological] wounds," Shinseki declared, "can be as debilitating as any physical battlefield trauma."

This is true. But gauging mental injury in the wake of war is not as straightforward as assessing, say, a lost limb or other physical damage. For example, at what point do we say that normal, if painful, readjustment difficulties have become so troubling as to qualify as a mental illness? How can clinicians predict which patients will recover when a veteran's odds of recovery depend so greatly on nonmedical factors, including his own expectations for recovery; social support available to him; and the intimate meaning he makes of his distress? Inevitably, successful caregiving will turn on a clear understanding of post-traumatic stress disorder.

One of the most important and paradoxical lessons to emerge from these insights is that lowering the threshold for receipt of disability benefits is not always in the best interest of the veteran and his family. Without question, some veterans will remain so irretrievably damaged by their war experience that they cannot participate in the competitive workplace. These men and women clearly deserve the roughly $2,300 monthly tax-free benefit (given for "total," or 100 percent, disability) and other resources the Veterans Administration offers. But what if disability entitlements actually work to the detriment of other patients by keeping them from meaningful work and by creating an incentive for them to embrace institutional dependence? And what if the system, well-intentioned though it surely is, does not adequately protect young veterans from a premature verdict of invalidism? Acknowledging and studying these effects of compensation can be politically delicate, yet doing do is essential to devising reentry programs of care for the nation's invisibly wounded warriors.

What Is PTSD

The most recent edition of the *Diagnostic and Statistical Manual (DSM IV)* of the American Psychiatric Association defines PTSD according to symptoms; their duration; and the nature of the "trauma" or event. Symptoms fall into three categories: re-experiencing (e.g., relentless nightmares; unbidden waking images; flashbacks); hyper-arousal (e.g., enhanced startle, anxiety, sleeplessness); and phobias (e.g., fear of driving after having been in a crash). These must persist for at least 30 days and impair function to some degree. Overwhelming calamity—or "stressor," as psychiatrists call it—of any kind, such as a natural disaster, rape, accident, or assault, can lead to PTSD.

Notably, not everyone who confronts horrific circumstances develops PTSD. Among the survivors of the Oklahoma City bombing, for example, 34 percent developed PTSD, according to a study by psychiatric epidemiologist Carol North. After a car accident or natural disaster, fewer than 10 percent of victims are affected, while among rape victims, well over half succumb. The reassuring news is that, as with grief and other emotional reactions to painful events, most sufferers get better with time, though periodic nightmares and easy startling may linger for additional months or even years.

In contrast to the sizeable literature on PTSD in civilian populations and in active-duty soldiers, data on veterans are harder to come by. To date, the congressionally mandated National Vietnam Veterans Readjustment Study (NVVRS) remains the landmark analysis. Data were collected during 1986 and 1987 and revealed that 15.2 percent of a random sample of veterans still met criteria for PTSD. Yet, a number of scholars found those estimates to be improbably high (e.g., if roughly one in six Vietnam veterans suffered from PTSD, as the NVVRS suggests, this would mean that virtually each and every soldier who served in combat—a ratio of 1 combatant to every 6 in support specialties—developed the condition). To help clarify the picture, a team of researchers from Columbia University undertook a reanalysis of the NVVRS. After their results appeared in *Science* in 2006, it became impossible for responsible researchers to consider the original findings of NVVRS as definitive.

According to the Columbia reanalysis, the psychological cost of the war was 40 percent lower than the original NVVRS estimate—that is, 9.1 percent were diagnosed with PTSD at the time of the study. The researchers arrived at this prevalence rate by considering information—collected by the original NVVRS investigators but not used—on veterans' functional impairment (i.e., their ability to hold a job, fulfill demands of family life, maintain friendships, etc). However, the Columbia team used a rather lenient definition of "impairment," stipulating that even veterans with "some difficulty" but who were "functioning pretty well" despite their symptoms had PTSD. This spurred yet another reanalysis. In a 2007 article in the *Journal of Traumatic Stress*, Harvard psychologist Richard McNally took the definition of impairment up a notch so that only veterans who had at least "moderate difficulty" in social or occupational functioning could qualify as having PTSD. In doing so, he further reduced the estimate of affliction to 5.4 percent. If nothing else, this analytic sequence—from the NVVRS, to the Columbia reevaluation, and to the McNally recalibration—serves as an object lesson in the definitional fluidity of psychiatric syndromes.

From the wars in Iraq and Afghanistan, researchers have collected data on thousands of active-duty servicemen, but very little on veterans of those conflicts. The most rigorous evaluation to date appeared in the *Archives of General Psychiatry* last summer. It was conducted by investigators at the Walter Reed Army Institute of Research who applied rigorous and uniform diagnostic standards. This distinguished their work from other studies on the current Gulf wars, which were deficient in one or more ways: failure to perform in-depth diagnostic assessments; use of broad sampling that did not distinguish combat from support personnel; or assessment by snapshot rather than longitudinal follow-up. The Walter Reed team assessed over 18,000 army soldiers in infantry brigade combat teams at three points: pre-deployment (to establish a baseline); three months after deployment; and at twelve months post-deployment. After three months the rate of PTSD (symptoms accompanied by "serious impairment") was 6.3 percent higher than the pre-deployment baseline. At a year, it was 7.3 percent higher.

The New VA Rule

On July 12, 2010, General Shinseki penned an op-ed in *USA Today* ("For Vets with PTSD, End of an Unfair Process") announcing a new Veterans Administration rule making it easier for veterans suffering from PTSD to file disability claims. Part of the rule was straightforward: The VA would no longer require that a veteran provide documentation of his exposure to combat trauma, seeing how such paperwork is often very difficult for veterans to obtain. Streamlining the lumbering claims bureaucracy is one thing, and welcome it is, but the new rule does not end there. It also establishes that noninfantry personnel can qualify for PTSD disability if they had good reason to fear danger, such as firefights or explosions, even if they did not actually experience it. "[If] a stressor claimed by a veteran is related to the veteran's fear of hostile military or terrorist activity, he is eligible for a PTSD benefits," according to the Federal Register. This is a strikingly novel amendment. The idea that one can sustain an enduring and disabling mental disorder based on anxious anticipation of a traumatic event that never materialized is a radical departure from the clinical—and common-sense—understanding that traumatic stress disorders are caused by events that actually do happen to people.[1] However, this is by no means the first time that controversy and ambiguity have swirled around the diagnosis of PTSD.

During the Civil War, some soldiers were said to suffer "irritable heart" or "Da Costa's Syndrome"—a condition marked by shortness of breath, chest discomfort, and pounding palpitations that doctors could not attribute to a medical cause. In World War I, the condition became known as "shell shock" and was characterized as a mental problem. The inability to cope was believed to reflect personal weakness—an underlying genetic or psychological vulnerability; combat itself, no matter how intense, was deemed little more than a precipitating factor. Otherwise well-adjusted individuals were believed to be at small risk of suffering more than a transient stress reaction once they were removed from the front.

In 1917, the British neuroanatomist Grafton Elliot Smith and the psychologist Tom Pear challenged this view. They attributed the cause more to the experiences of war and less to the character or fiber of soldiers themselves. "Psychoneurosis may be produced in almost anyone if only his environment be made 'difficult' enough for him," they wrote in their book, *Shell Shock and Its Lessons*. This triggered a feisty debate within British military psychiatry, and eventually the two sides came to agree that both the soldier's predisposition to stress and his exposure to hostilities contributed to breakdown. By World War II, then, military psychiatrists believed that even the bravest and fittest soldier could endure only so much. "Every man has his breaking point," the saying went.

The story of PTSD, as we know it today, starts with the Vietnam War. In the late 1960s, a band of self-described anti-war psychiatrists—led by Chaim Shatan and Robert Jay Lifton, who was well known for his work on the psychological damage wrought by Hiroshima—formulated a new diagnostic concept to describe the psychological wounds that the veterans sustained in the war. They called it "Post-Vietnam Syndrome," a disorder marked by "growing apathy, cynicism, alienation, depression, mistrust, and expectation of betrayal as well as an inability to concentrate, insomnia, nightmares, restlessness, uprootedness, and impatience with almost any job or course of study." Not uncommonly, the psychiatrists said, these symptoms did not emerge until months or years after the veterans returned home. Civilian contempt for veterans, according to Messrs. Shatan and Lifton, further entrenched their hostility and impeded their return.

This vision inspired portrayals of the Vietnam veteran as a kind of "walking time bomb," "living wreckage," or rampaging loner, images immortalized in films such as "Taxi Driver" and "Rambo." In the summer of 1972, the *New York Times* ran a front-page story on Post-Vietnam Syndrome. It reported that 50 percent of all Vietnam veterans—not just combat veterans—needed professional help to readjust, and contained phrases such as "psychiatric casualty," "emotionally disturbed," and "men with damaged brains." By contrast, veterans of World War II were heralded as heroes. They had fought in a popular war, a vital distinction for understanding how veterans and the public give meaning to their wartime hardships and sacrifice.

Historians and sociologists note that the high-profile involvement of civilian psychiatrists in the wake of the Vietnam War was another feature that set those returning soldiers apart. "The suggestion or outright assertion was that Vietnam veterans have been unique in American history for their psychiatric problems," writes the historian Eric T. Dean Jr. in *Shook over Hell: Post-Traumatic Stress, Vietnam, and the Civil War*. As the image of the psychologically injured veteran took root in the national conscience, the psychiatric profession debated the wisdom of giving him his own diagnosis.

PTSD Becomes Official

In 1980, the American Psychiatric Association adopted post-traumatic stress disorder (rather than the narrower post-Vietnam syndrome) as an official diagnosis in the third edition of its *Diagnostic and Statistical Manual*. A patient could be diagnosed with PTSD if he experienced a trauma or "stressor" that, as DSM described it, would "evoke significant symptoms of distress in almost everyone." Rape, combat, torture, and fires were those deemed to fall, as the DSM III required, "generally outside the range of usual human experience." Thus, while the stress was unusual, the development of PTSD in its wake was not.

No longer were prolonged traumatic reactions viewed as a reflection of an individual's constitutional vulnerability. Instead, stress-induced syndromes were a natural process of adapting to extreme stress. With the introduction of PTSD into the psychiatric manual, the single-minded emphasis on the importance of one's pre-morbid state in shaping response to crisis gave way to preoccupation with the trauma itself and its supposed leveling effect on human response. Surely, it was wrong of earlier psychiatrists to attribute war-related pathology solely to the combatant himself, but the DSM III definition embodied an equal but opposite error: It obliterated the role of an individual's own characteristics in the development of the condition. Not surprising, perhaps, this blunder served a political purpose. As British psychiatrist Derek Summerfield put it, the newly minted diagnosis of PTSD "was meant to shift the focus of attention from the details of a soldier's background and psyche to the fundamentally traumatic nature of war."

Shatan and Lifton clearly saw PTSD as a normal response. "The placement of post-traumatic stress disorder in [the DSM] allows us to see the policies of diagnosis and disease in an especially clear light," writes combat veteran and sociologist Wilbur Scott in his detailed 1993 account *The Politics of Readjustment: Vietnam Veterans Since the War*. The diagnosis of PTSD is in the DSM, Mr. Scott writes, "because a core of psychiatrists and Vietnam veterans worked conscientiously and deliberately for years to put it there . . . at issue was the question of what constitutes a normal reaction or experience of soldiers to combat." Thus, by the time PTSD was incorporated into the official psychiatric lexicon, it bore a hybrid legacy— part political artifact of the antiwar movement, part legitimate diagnosis.

Over the years, the major symptoms of PTSD have remained fairly straightforward—re-experiencing, anxiety, and phobic avoidance—but what counted as a traumatic experience turned out to be a moving target in subsequent editions of the DSM. In 1987, the DSM III was revised to expand the definition of a traumatic experience. The concept of stressor now included witnessing harm to others, such as a horrific car accident in progress. In the fourth edition in 1994, the range of "traumatic" events was expanded further to include hearing about harm or threats to others, such as the unexpected death of a loved one or receiving a fatal diagnosis such as terminal cancer oneself. No longer did one need to experience a life-threatening situation directly or be a close witness to a ghastly accident or atrocity. As long as one experienced an "intense fear, helplessness, or horror" in response to a catastrophic event (e.g., after watching the September 11 terrorist attacks on television, or being in a minor car accident) he could conceivably qualify for a diagnosis of PTSD if symptoms of re-experiencing, arousal, and phobias persisted for a month.

There is pitched debate within the field of traumatology as to whether a stressor should be defined as whatever traumatizes a person. True, a person might feel "traumatized" by, say, a minor car accident—but to say that a fender-bender counts as trauma alongside such horrors as concentration camps, rape, or the Bataan Death March is to dilute the concept. "A great deal rides on how we define the concept of traumatic stressor," says Richard J. McNally. In the civilian realm, he says, "the more we broaden the category of traumatic stressors, the less credibly we can assign causal significance to a given stressor itself and the more weight we must place on personal vulnerability." In the context of war, too, while anticipatory fear of being thrust in harm's way could conceivably morph into a crippling stress reaction, this will almost surely be more likely among individuals who struggled with anxiety-related problems prior to deployment. Surely, their distress merits treatment from military psychiatrists, but the odds that such symptoms persist after separation from the military, let alone harden into a serious, lasting state of disablement, are probably very low.

The Troubled VA Disability System

Secretary Shinseki's move to reduce the bureaucratic hurdles to the VA disability system and broaden eligibility for PTSD will add to the already accelerating stream of veterans who are applying to enter it. Thus, it is imperative that the VA turn its attention to that system itself. Two overarching problems need remedies. The first is the culture of clinical diagnosis. Some disability evaluators now use a detailed interview checklist to gauge the degree to which daily function is impaired, but its implementation is uneven across medical centers. Thus, it is still easy for clinicians—especially those whose diagnostic skills were honed during the Vietnam era—to label problems such as anxiety, guilt over comrades who died, and chronic sleep disturbance mental illnesses. This is facile, of course, as symptoms splay out along a continuum ranging from normal, if painful, readjustment difficulties to chronic, debilitating pathology. Further, not all symptoms of distress in someone who has been to war reflexively signal the presence of PTSD, as some clinicians seem to think. Among veterans whose problems are indeed war-related, however, the distinction between reversible and lasting incapacitation matters greatly when the veteran is seeking disability status. And this brings us to the second matter; the inadvertent damage that disability benefits themselves can sometimes cause.

Imagine a young soldier wounded in Afghanistan. His physical injuries heal, but his mind remains tormented. Sudden noises make him jump out of his skin. He is flooded with memories of a bloody firefight, tormented by nightmares, can barely concentrate, and feels emotionally detached from everything and everybody. At 23 years old, the soldier is about to be discharged from the military. Fearing he'll never be able to hold a job or fully function in society he applies for "total" disability (the maximum designation, which provides roughly $2,300 per month) compensation for PTSD from the VA. This soldier has resigned himself to a life of chronic mental illness. On its face, this seems only logical, and granting the benefits seems humane. But in reality it is probably the last thing the young soldier-turning-veteran needs—because compensation will confirm his fears that he is indeed beyond recovery.

While a sad verdict for anyone, it is especially tragic for someone only in his twenties. Injured soldiers can apply for and receive VA disability benefits even before they have been discharged from the military—and, remarkably, before they have even been given the psychiatric treatment that could help them considerably. Imagine telling someone with a spinal injury that he'll never walk again—before he has had surgery and physical therapy. A rush to judgment about the prognosis of psychic injuries carries serious long-term consequences insofar as a veteran who is unwittingly encouraged to see himself as beyond repair risks fulfilling that prophecy. Why should I bother with treatment? he might think. A terrible mistake, of course. The months before and after separation from the service are periods when mental wounds are fresh and thus most responsive to therapeutic intervention, including medication.

Told he is disabled, the veteran and his family may assume—often incorrectly—that he is no longer able to work. At home on disability, he risks adopting a "sick role" that ends up depriving him of the estimable therapeutic value of work. Lost are the sense of purpose work gives (or at least the distraction from depressive rumination it provides), the daily structure it affords, and the opportunity for socializing and cultivating friendships. The longer he is unemployed, the more his confidence in his ability and motivation to work erodes and his skills atrophy. Once a patient is caught in such a downward spiral of invalidism, it can be hard to throttle back out. What's more, compensation contingent upon being sick often creates a perverse incentive to remain sick. For example, even if a veteran wants very much to work, he understandably fears losing his financial safety net if he leaves the disability rolls to take a job that ends up proving too much for him. This is how full disability status can undermine the possibility of recovery.

What To Do: Treatment First

For many veterans, the transition between military and civilian life is a critical juncture marked by acute feelings of flux and dislocation. Recall the scene in *The Hurt Locker* (one of the few scenes, incidentally, that former soldiers have deemed realistic) in which Sergeant William James stares at the wall of cereal boxes in the supermarket, disoriented by the tranquil and often trivial nature of the civilian world. As Sebastian Junger wrote in his powerful book *War*, "Some of the men worry they'll never again be satisfied with a 'normal life' . . . They worry that they may have been ruined for anything else."

Returning from war is a major existential project. Imparting meaning to the wartime experience, reconfiguring personal identity, and reimagining one's future take time. Sometimes the emotional intensity can be overwhelming—especially when coupled with nightmares and high anxiety or depression—and even warrants professional help. When this happens, the veteran should receive a message of promise and hope. This means a prescription for quality treatment and rehabilitation—ideally before the patient is even permitted to apply for disability status. However, under the current system, when a veteran files a disability claim, a ratings examiner is assigned to determine the extent of incapacitation, irrespective of whether he has first received care.

As part of the assessment, the examiner requests a psychiatric evaluation with a psychiatrist or a psychologist to obtain a diagnosis. If the veteran is diagnosed with PTSD by the clinician, the ratings examiner then assigns a severity index to his disability. The Veterans Benefits Administration recognizes different levels of disability. As detailed in the Code of Federal Regulations, a ten percent severity rating for a mental illness denotes "mild or transient symptoms which [affect] occupational tasks only during periods of significant stress." A patient assigned 30 percent disability has "intermittent periods of inability to perform occupational tasks although generally functioning satisfactorily." A 50 percent rating begins to denote significant deficits including "difficulty in understanding complex commands" and reduced reliability and productivity. The most severe level, 100 percent, corresponds to "total occupational and social impairment."

Something is terribly wrong with this picture. To conclude that a veteran has dismal prospects for meaningful recovery before he or she has had a course of therapy and rehabilitation is premature in the extreme.[2] To be sure, the VA is trying hard to make treatment accessible, but administrators, raters, and clinicians cannot require patients to accept it as a condition of being considered for disability compensation. Absent a course of quality treatment and rehabilitation, evaluators simply do not have enough evidence to make a determination. Unwittingly, this policy has set in motion a growing dependence on the VA and disincentive to meaningful improvement. In 2008, Senator Richard Burr of North Carolina, the ranking member of the Senate Veterans Affairs Committee, sought a limited remedy. He introduced the Veterans Mental Health Treatment First Act. The purpose of this bill was to induce new veterans to embark upon a path to recovery. Any veteran diagnosed with major depression, post-traumatic stress disorder, or other anxiety disorders stemming from military activity would be eligible for a financial incentive (which Burr called a "wellness stipend") to adhere to an individualized course of treatment and agree to a pause in claims action for at least a year or until completion of treatment, which ever came first. The bill died in committee.

Don't Fight the Same War Twice

Mental health experts have learned a lot about how not to treat veterans from our experience during the Vietnam era. I speak from my experience as a psychiatrist at the West Haven Veterans Affairs Medical Center in Connecticut from 1988 to

1992, a time of blossoming interest in PTSD within both the VA and the mental-health establishment. Good intentions were abundant, but, in retrospect, much of our treatment philosophy was misguided. For example, clinicians tended to view whatever problem beset a veteran as a product of his war experience. In addition, therapists spent too much time urging veterans to experience catharsis by reliving their war experiences in group therapy, individual therapy, art therapy, and theatre reenactments. Groups of twenty or so veterans were admitted to the hospital and stayed together, platoonlike, for four months. This practice took them out of their communities and away from their families. I remember some of the men coming back from a day's leave from the hospital ward with new war-themed tattoos and combat fatigues—not exactly readjustment! It is clear, in retrospect, that instead of fostering regression, we should have emphasized resolution of everyday problems of living, such as family chaos, employment difficulties, and substance abuse.

The good news is that most of these inpatient programs are now shuttered. Studies showed them to be largely ineffective. What followed over the years was a wholesale shift away from cathartic reenactment of war trauma and a growing emphasis on forward-looking rehabilitation and evidence-based treatments such as cognitive therapy, behavioral desensitization (some techniques involving virtual reality recreations of combat scenarios), and medication if needed. The VA does appear to be making serious efforts to ensure that all mental health clinics are equipped to offer state of the art treatment for PTSD.

Some clinicians, myself included, would even like to see the diagnosis of PTSD downplayed altogether in favor of trying to understand patients' symptoms in context. As Texas psychiatrist Martha Leatherman puts it, "behaviors such as easy startling, hypervigilance, and sleep disturbance that are common in combat situations are normal, survival mechanisms," she says. Unfortunately, when they return, veterans are told that these symptoms mean PTSD. "This stirs up visions of Vietnam veterans living under bridges," Leatherman says, "and then, in a panic, they apply for disability compensation for PTSD so that they won't end up homeless too." Regrettably, the legacy of Vietnam era PTSD haunts the current generation of veterans. "It has been very troubling to me to see OEF/OIF veterans who truly need mental health treatment refuse it because it would mean having an illness that is associated with Vietnam-era chronicity and thus is incurable." The clinicians' job, of course, is not to incite morbid preoccupations, but to dispel misconceptions about Vietnam veterans (the vast majority of whom went on to function well) and steer veterans, as early as possible, to healthier interpretations of their symptoms. Early intervention also leverages the well-established fact that prognosis after trauma greatly depends on what happens to the individual in its immediate wake. That is why serious attention must be paid to the everyday problems that beset many veterans during the readjustment period, such as financial stress, marital discord, parenting strains, occupational needs.[3]

Finally, the balkanization of the veteran's services complex demands attention. The federal Veterans Benefits Administration (VBA) and the Veterans Health Administration (VHA) tend to operate in separate universes. The VBA is geared toward helping veterans maximize benefits and gives little to no attention to improving their clinical situation. On the other hand, the VHA is focused on treatment, as it should be, but doesn't extend its expertise to helping veterans with the financial hardships they face. (These can be the kinds of problems that might lead a patient to turn to disability compensation—not because he is incapable of work but because the reliable check is a rational solution to his financial woes.) County-based Veterans Service Officers actively help veterans file for disability—not necessarily a bad thing at all, but because they are advocates, their job is to get a veteran what he wants, which is not necessarily in his best clinical interest. Lastly, the Veteran Service Organizations which, as a matter of principle, are driven to funnel largesse to their constituents, tend to be extremely suspicious of proposed reforms of the disability system as they were of Senator Burr's proposal. With the missions of both agencies and the agendas of pressure groups all working at cross purposes, disability reform is a daunting challenge indeed.

Anyone who fights in a war is changed by it, but few are irreparably damaged. For those who never regain their civilian footing despite the best treatment, full and generous disability compensation is their due. Otherwise, it is reckless to allow a young veteran to surrender to his psychological wounds without first urging him to pursue recovery.

Over the last hundred years or so, psychiatry has taken very different perspectives on war stress: from an overly harsh, blame-the-soldier stance in World War I, to the healthy recognition in World War II that even the most psychologically healthy individual can develop war-related symptoms, to the misguided expectation in the wake of Vietnam that lasting PTSD was routine. The new VA rule, which expands PTSD disability eligibility to noncombatants who have experienced the dread of harm but have not had an actual encounter with it, alters the meaning yet again. What should have been a welcome bureaucratic reform by the VA—waiving documentation that might be difficult or impossible to obtain—ended up distorting the diagnosis. Add to this the practice of conferring disability status upon a veteran before his prospects for recovery are known, and the long journey home will now be harder than it already is.

Notes

1. The new rule is actually quite confusing. See the *Federal Register*, 75:133 (July 13, 2010), 39847, available online at

http://www.thefederalregister.com/d.p/2010-07-13-2010-16885. (This and subsequent weblinks accessed December 13, 2010.) While the *Federal Register* states that a diagnosis of PTSD cannot be made "in the absence of exposure to a traumatic event," in keeping with the formal psychiatric conception of PTSD, it also says, apparently contrarily, that "constant vigilance against unexpected attack" can constitute a stressor and that PTSD can result from "veteran's fear of hostile military or terrorist activity."

2. Studies of Vietnam veterans have found that 68 to 94 percent of claimants seeking treatment for the first time are also applying for PTSD disability benefits; for review see B. Christopher Frueh, et al., "Disability compensation seeking among veterans evaluated for posttraumatic stress disorder," *Psychiatric Services* 54 (January 2003), 84–91. According to Nina Sayer and colleagues, "most claimants reported seeking disability compensation for symbolic reasons, especially for acknowledgement, validation and relief from self-blame; see Nina Sayer, et al., "Veterans seeking disability benefits for post-traumatic stress disorder: Who applies and the self-reported meaning of disability compensation," *Social Science & Medicine* 58:11 (June 2004), 2133–43. I could not find comparable studies on OIE and OIF veterans, but the Compensation and Pension examiners I interviewed suggest that the "disability first" approach is not uncommon.

3. The problem of fraud, too, cannot be overlooked. See B. Christopher Frueh, et al., "US Department of Veterans Affairs disability policies for PTSD: Administrative trends and implications for treatment, rehabilitation, and research," *American Journal of Public Health* 97:12 (December 2007), 2143–2145; see also Gail Poyner, "Psychological Evaluations of Veterans Claiming PTSD Disability with the Department of Veterans Affairs: A Clinician's Viewpoint," *Psychological Injury and Law* 3:2 (2010), 130–2. Poyner, who had received praise from VA personnel for her careful diagnostic evalua-

tions, was told by the VA in 2009 that her services were no longer needed after she began using approved psychological tests to distinguish between veterans who were claiming to have PTSD when they did not and those whose complaints were clinically authentic.

Periodical and Internet Sources Bibliography

The following articles have been selected to supplement the diverse views presented in this chapter.

Tony Bateson	"Mercury, Vaccines, and Autism," *Age of Autism*, November 8, 2012. www.ageofautism.com.
Tony Dokoupil	"A New Theory of PTSD and Veterans: Moral Injury," *Newsweek*, December 3, 2012.
Katherine Ellison	"Brain Scans Link ADHD to Biological Flaw Tied to Motivation," *Washington Post*, September 22, 2009.
Amanda Gardner	"Depression, PTSD Plagues Many Iraq Vets," CNN.com, June 7, 2010. www.cnn.com.
Patricia Kime	"Families: Vets' PTSD 'Like Living in Hell,'" *Marine Corps Times*, February 11, 2012.
Nan Levinson	"Understanding a New Era of PTSD," *Mother Jones*, June 28, 2012.
Caroline Miller	"Do Video Games Cause ADHD?," Child Mind Institute, July 31, 2012. www.childmind.org.
Seth Mnookin	"The Autism Vaccine Controversy and the Need for Responsible Science Journalism," *Huffington Post*, January 5, 2012. www.huffingtonpost.com.
Ian Sample	"ADHD: Genes Play a Role, but How Crucial Are They?," *The Guardian* (UK), October 2, 2010.
Dave Tombers	"Do Vaccines Really Cause Autism?," WND, May 4, 2012. www.wnd.com.
Emily Willingham	"Influenza, Fever, and Autism: How Much Should You Worry?," *Forbes*, November 12, 2012.

OPPOSING
VIEWPOINTS®
SERIES

CHAPTER 3

How Should Behavioral Disorders Be Treated?

Chapter Preface

Funded by the US Army Medical Research and Material Command, virtual reality exposure therapy (VRET) is being studied by the National Center for Telehealth and Technology (T2) to treat Iraq and Afghanistan veterans with post-traumatic stress disorder (PTSD). Various types of "VR trainers" are used in ninety-minute treatment sessions, depending on the scenario. If an attack took place while driving, a soldier wears a headset re-creating a 360° interactive simulation of the environment and navigates with a joystick that mimics the sensation of steering a combat vehicle. For a situation on foot, a soldier stands on a vibrating platform and holds a mock assault rifle. Synthesized odors of burning rubber and firing weapons are sprayed into the air to complete the sensory experience. "The whole treatment is customized to their memory, down to the day, time, weather conditions, location in the convoy, and the combat stimuli themselves," states Greg Reger, lead psychologist for T2. "The purpose is to activate the experience to increase emotional engagement, so they can process that memory," he explains.

VRET makes use of cutting-edge computer technology to generate reenactments as realistically as possible. While it was first introduced in 1997 with Virtual Vietnam, clinical psychologist Albert Rizzo developed VRET as it is known today, drawing innovations from "Full Spectrum Warrior," a game used for training by the US Department of Defense. "We use gaming software to create realistic combat environments. We are bringing the war home so we can treat our wounded service members," Rizzo explains, adding, "They have gone through and seen horrible things so it's not easy for them to revisit."

In the T2 study, VRET is being compared with traditional "imaginal" exposure therapy, in which a patient imagines memories of a trauma in detail and verbally describes them to gain control over related anxieties. "Consider the difference between someone closing his eyes and imagining the situation versus someone who tells his story while the same type of event is occurring with the sights and sounds—it is so much more emotionally engaging," asserts Reger. Furthermore, this high-tech approach is thought to attract younger troops—a group accustomed to technology in their everyday lives—who may be resistant to talk therapy. "You have a generation of soldiers, Marines, and service members who grew up in a digital world, who have played thousands of hours of computer games," says Rizzo. "That is the group you may be able to appeal to and get them to come in and get treatment."

The authors of the viewpoints in the following chapter give their opinions on how behavioral disorders, including PTSD, can or should be treated.

| "*Stimulant medication deserves to be the first line treatment [for ADHD].*"

Drugs Are an Effective Treatment for Attention-Deficit/Hyperactivity Disorder

Caroline Miller

In the following viewpoint, Caroline Miller advocates the use of medication to treat children with attention-deficit/hyperactivity disorder (ADHD). The biggest long-term study, the author states, demonstrates that medication reduced symptoms better than behavioral therapy, which did not significantly improve outcomes when added to medication. Whether children develop tolerance for the prescribed stimulants, Miller notes, remains an area of disagreement. But when tolerance does occur, she maintains, numerous experts conclude that medication is still valuable and improves the lives of children with ADHD.

    Caroline Miller is editorial director of the Child Mind Institute, an organization focused on childhood psychiatric and learning disabilities.

As you read, consider the following questions:

1. What does Miller say about people who argue that parents of kids with ADHD overmedicate?

2. What reason does Alan Ravitz, as cited by the author, provide for an increase in ADHD medication that does not imply tolerance?

3. How does Michael Milham, as cited by Miller, respond to the problem of tolerance to medication in treating ADHD?

Passions are running high on the issue of medication for kids with ADHD [attention-deficit/hyperactivity disorder]. We've seen a series of very emotional articles recently charging that too many kids are being diagnosed with the disorder—if it is a disorder at all—and especially that too many kids are being medicated.

It can be very disturbing for parents to be told they're overmedicating kids, especially by people who seem to have little direct experience with the medication—or the kids it's being prescribed to.

Because this has become a controversial issue, it's worth taking the time to examine what we really do *know* about ADHD and the effectiveness of medication. Is there sound scientific evidence about whether it works and whether it continues to work over time?

The MTA Study

The biggest long-term study of treatment for children with ADHD, called the MTA [Multimodal Treatment Study of Children with ADHD] study, treated nearly 600 children in the late 1990s for 14 months, to compare the effectiveness of several different protocols—medication, behavioral treatment, or both. That study showed clearly that medication reduced symptoms more effectively than behavioral therapies, and that adding the behavioral interventions didn't improve the result significantly over medication alone.

The MTA study showed that "stimulant medication deserves to be the first line treatment based on efficacy," as Dr.

James Swanson, one of the study's authors, puts it, "when a family is concerned about the well-being of a child with ADHD tomorrow—or next month or next year." Dr. Swanson, a psychologist, is a prominent researcher in the field of ADHD and director of the Child Development Center at the University of California, Irvine, School of Medicine. This is generally accepted by members of the psychiatric community and other ADHD experts, and the results have been replicated in other, smaller studies that lasted as long as two years.

But there is less agreement on a related issue, which is whether kids develop tolerance to stimulant medications over time, and therefore need an increased dosage to get the same effect.

At the beginning of the MTA study, the optimum dosage of methylphenidate (the active ingredient in Ritalin) for each child was determined individually, and very methodically, over the course of the first month. Nonetheless, during the following 13 months of treatment there was pattern of kids needing increased doses to continue to get the same effect, Swanson reports. In a follow-up analysis of the findings, Swanson writes that a dose increase was required in 54% of the medication-only group, with the dose per unit of body weight increasing on average 19%.

Roughly the same finding appears in a two-year study published in 2005 of more than 200 kids on Concerta, a delayed-release form of methylphenidate. The effectiveness of the medication was maintained successfully through the second year, but the dosage was increased an average of 15% per unit of body weight.

This finding reflects the experience of some clinicians. Dr. Roy Boorady, a Child Mind Institute psychiatrist who's been treating kids with ADHD for more than 15 years, says he often increases the dosage within the first several years of treating a child. "When I treat a child from, say, age seven, I find I have to increase dose, maybe 20%, to recapture the benefit.

But after 15 or 16, I find that kids end up needing less, not more." Dr. Boorady notes that this may be the result of ADHD symptoms waning, as they often do, in late adolescence, and it's also the case that as the teenagers' livers mature, they may be able to metabolize the medication more efficiently.

Another Reason for Increasing Dosage

But not all clinicians report the same effect. Dr. Alan Ravitz, another veteran child and adolescent psychiatrist now at the Child Mind Institute, notes that there could be other reasons for common increases in dosage over the years that don't imply tolerance: As a child gets older he faces increased expectations in school, higher demand for concentration. The child gets more aware of what the medication does and might want more of that feeling. He may be more tuned in to what other kids are doing, and feel competitive. Dr. Ravitz notes that he sees lots of patients who are adults and he does not typically need to increase the dose over the span of many years.

Dr. Rachel Klein, a clinician and researcher at New York University, also says she sees no pattern of needing to increase doses for kids with ADHD. Dr. Klein was one of the authors of a study published in 2004 in which 103 children with ADHD underwent treatment for two years, and they found no erosion of the benefit over time, Dr. Klein notes. As with the MTA study, no significant academic or behavioral improvement was gained by adding other psychosocial interventions to the medication regimen. "Significant benefits from methylphenidate were stable over two years," the authors wrote.

Dr. Klein acknowledges that there are shifts in an individual child's responsiveness to stimulant medications, but says there is no demonstrated pattern of diminished response. "It may happen in some cases," she says. "I've seen kids who lose the effect, and I've seen kids who didn't respond at one time and respond two years later. So there's variation, but on average that's not true."

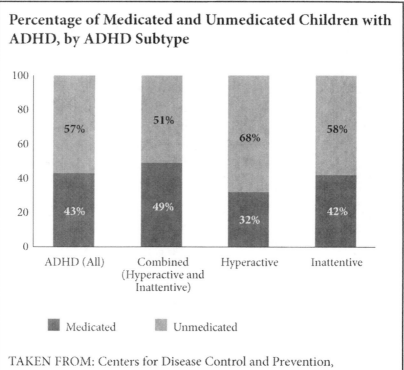

Percentage of Medicated and Unmedicated Children with ADHD, by ADHD Subtype

TAKEN FROM: Centers for Disease Control and Prevention, "PLAY Study Findings (Project to Learn about ADHD in Youth)," September 28, 2012. www.cdc.gov.

The Brain Is Adjusting

In children who do need increased doses to maintain effectiveness, it's plausible that what's at work is the brain adjusting to the stimulant, which works by increasing the dopamine level in the brain, Swanson and others note. The brain could adjust by producing more receptors or more sensitivity in the receptors that remove dopamine from the system.

There is clear evidence that something like this happens, to some children, over a day of taking medication. Swanson and other researchers documented this effect, called acute tolerance, in a study published in 1999: Over the course of a day of continuous medication, kids need a higher dose in the afternoon to deliver the same effect as a smaller does in the morning. This insight led to the development of ascending-dose stimulant medications like Concerta, which delivers methylphenidate at the rate of 30% in the morning and 70% in the afternoon.

Does this suggest that a similar adjustment might be made over a period of months and years—one that doesn't disappear when the medication leaves the body at night? "It's certainly plausible that there is tolerance developing very slowly over time," says Dr. Stephen Hinshaw, another one of the authors of the MTA study: "We just don't know if what happens on the scale of 12 hours happens over 12 years. We just don't know."

Dr. Hinshaw, professor of psychology at the University of California, Berkeley, notes that sometimes after years of effective treatment, a patient with ADHD needs to switch to a different medication, say from Concerta (methylphenidate) to Adderall (amphetamine) to maintain the effect.

The Long-Term Effectiveness of Medications

One source of confusion in the discussion of long-term effectiveness of ADHD medications is a long-term follow-up to the 14-month MTA study, which checked in with participants periodically after they were no longer being treated as part of the study. Kids in the MTA study who were in the medications group, when contacted later, had lost half the benefit by the end of two years, and all of it by the end of three years.

Dr. Swanson, one of the authors of the follow-up analysis, notes that the dwindling benefit was seen not only in the whole group—many, if not most of whom had abandoned the treatment with medication—but within the subgroup of kids whose parents continued with medication. He sees that as evidence of tolerance developing. Dr. L. Alan Sroufe, writing in a widely circulated piece in the *New York Times*, used this MTA follow-up analysis to argue that stimulant medications had been shown to have no long-term value.

But Dr. Hinshaw and others disagree. Dr. Hinshaw notes that the MTA follow-up was what researchers call a "naturalistic" follow-up: it's not controlled, and the treatment kids received from practitioners in their communities wasn't standardized in any way. It's not scientifically meaningful, Dr. Hinshaw and others argue, and the decline in results from medication could just as well reflect the fact that the medication wasn't managed well.

During the original 14 months, the titration [a measurement of exact volume] was specific to each child, each participant saw a doctor once a month for a 20-minute visit, 10 minutes of which was "alone time" with the doctor, and the doctor also spoke to the child's teacher to monitor his progress once a month. Community care, Dr. Hinshaw notes, often means you see a pediatrician once every five months, there is no communication with teachers, and no expert titration. The level of care just isn't similar to that in the study.

Also, Dr. Hinshaw notes, when you're in a naturalistic phase the children who continue to get medication are an admixture of upper-middle-class kids whose families can afford more treatment and families whose kids have very severe symptoms. These biases invalidate the value of the follow-up data.

"That's not an experimental study," Dr. Klein says. "We don't know that the kids actually stayed on meds. Was the dosage properly monitored? Those who stayed on the medications the longest may have been the ones most severely impacted by their symptoms. What we know is that when you do control the treatment it works over time."

Treatment Is Effective Despite Tolerance

The larger issue raised by this disagreement is whether the possibility of brain adaptation to medication for ADHD undermines [medications'] effectiveness.

Dr. Swanson concludes that evidence of tolerance is problematic for long-term use. "Dose increases are an effective strategy to overcome this loss, at least in the first one or two years of treatment," he writes. "However, this may not be a viable long term strategy for the majority of ADHD youth prescribed CNS [central nervous system] stimulants."

His concern is underscored by two other recent studies based on brain scans that suggest that use of stimulant medications may increase the density of what are called dopamine transporters (DAT), which are the primary target of stimulants like methylphenidate. The studies were led by Dr. Gene-Jack Wang, a neuroscientist and chair of Brookhaven National Laboratory's Medical Department, and Dr. Nora Volkow, a psychiatrist and scientist who is director of the National Institute on Drug Abuse (NIDA) at the National Institutes of Health. Brain scans of children who had been on methylphenidate for a year showed an increased density of transporters, which they hypothesize could correspond with a declining clinical effect of the medication on ADHD symptoms. Meta-analysis of other studies, adds Dr. Swanson, also showed a strong association between prior stimulant exposure and DAT density.

What Dr. Swanson and others agree on is that the possibility of developing tolerance over the long term doesn't undermine the value of medication for children with ADHD in the short run, when it may very significantly improve their lives.

As Dr. Michael Milham, a neuroscience researcher and child psychiatrist at the Child Mind Institute, puts it: "If some kids do develop tolerance to the medication, *so what?* Lots of good medications become ineffective eventually, from SSRIs [selective serotonin reuptake inhibitors] to blood pressure medications. That doesn't mean we don't use them for as long as they work."

Swanson concurs: "We don't need to justify giving medication to kids based on what it's going to do 10 years from now. The parent comes to us with a child who is getting kicked out of school. A child who doesn't have any friends. The parent wants to know, what can we do *now*—for the next year of my child's life? Medication's going to be the best treatment. And that's complete justification for giving it."

| "With the expanded and extended use of stimulants [to treat ADHD] comes mounting concern that the drugs might take a toll on the brain over the long run."

Do ADHD Drugs Take a Toll on the Brain?

Edmund S. Higgins

Edmund S. Higgins is a clinical assistant professor of family medicine and psychiatry at the Medical University of South Carolina. In the following viewpoint, Higgins argues that stimulants prescribed for attention-deficit/hyperactivity disorder (ADHD) may have long-term adverse effects. Numerous animal studies reveal that methylphenidate (the active ingredient in Ritalin and Concerta) and amphetamine (the active ingredient in Adderall) could change the brain's structures and functions, the author reports, resulting in depression, anxiety, and, paradoxically, cognitive deficits. Furthermore, these stimulants raise concerns of addiction as well as possible links to Parkinson's disease and stunted growth in children, he maintains. Therefore, Higgins encourages the adoption of several measures to restrict or reduce the use of stimulants to treat ADHD.

As you read, consider the following questions:

1. What trend does Higgins say accounts for the prescription of stimulants to a growing number of patients with moderate to mild inattention?

2. As reported by the author, what resulted in an experiment with rats that received doses of methylphenidate similarly prescribed to children?

3. What did a recent experiment in animals discover about methylphenidate and the brain, as described by Higgins?

A few years ago a single mother who had recently moved to town came to my office asking me to prescribe the stimulant drug Adderall for her sixth-grade son. The boy had been taking the medication for several years, and his mother had liked its effects: it made homework time easier and improved her son's grades.

At the time of this visit, the boy was off the medication, and I conducted a series of cognitive and behavioral tests on him. He performed wonderfully. I also noticed that off the medication he was friendly and playful. On a previous casual encounter, when the boy had been on Adderall, he had seemed reserved and quiet. His mother acknowledged this was a side effect of the Adderall. I told her that I did not think her son had attention-deficit hyperactivity disorder (ADHD) and that he did not need medication. That was the last time I saw her.

Attention-deficit/hyperactivity disorder afflicts about 5 percent of U.S. children—twice as many boys as girls—age six to 17, according to a recent survey conducted by the Centers for Disease Control and Prevention [CDC]. As its name implies, people with the condition have trouble focusing and often are hyperactive or impulsive. An estimated 9 percent of boys and 4 percent of girls in the U.S. are taking stimulant medications as part of their therapy for ADHD, the CDC reported in 2005. The majority of patients take methylphenidate

(Ritalin, Concerta), whereas most of the rest are prescribed an amphetamine such as Adderall.

Although it sounds counterintuitive to give stimulants to a person who is hyperactive, these drugs are thought to boost activity in the parts of the brain responsible for attention and self-control. Indeed, the pills can improve attention, concentration and productivity and also suppress impulsive behavior, producing significant improvements in some people's lives. Severe inattention and impulsivity put individuals at risk for substance abuse, unemployment, crime and car accidents. Thus, appropriate medication might keep a person out of prison, away from addictive drugs or in a job.

Over the past 15 years, however, doctors have been pinning the ADHD label on—and prescribing stimulants for—a rapidly rising number of patients, including those with moderate to mild inattention, some of whom, like the sixth grader I saw, have a normal ability to focus. This trend may be fueled in part by a relaxation of official diagnostic criteria for the disorder, combined with a lower tolerance in society for mild behavioral or cognitive problems.

In addition, patients are no longer just taking the medicines for a few years during grade school but are encouraged to stay on them into adulthood. In 2008 two new stimulants—Vyvanse (amphetamine) and Concerta—received U.S. Food and Drug Administration indications for treating adults, and pharmaceutical firms are pushing awareness of the adult forms of the disorder. What is more, many people who have no cognitive deficits are opting to take these drugs to boost their academic performance. A number of my patients—doctors, lawyers and other professionals—have asked me for stimulants in hopes of boosting their productivity. As a result of these developments, prescriptions for methylphenidate and amphetamine rose by almost 12 percent a year between 2000 and 2005, according to a 2007 study.

With the expanded and extended use of stimulants comes mounting concern that the drugs might take a toll on the brain over the long run. Indeed, a smattering of recent studies, most of them involving animals, hint that stimulants could alter the structure and function of the brain in ways that may depress mood, boost anxiety and, contrary to their short-term effects, lead to cognitive deficits. Human studies already indicate the medications can adversely affect areas of the brain that govern growth in children, and some researchers worry that additional harms have yet to be unearthed.

Medicine for the Mind

To appreciate why stimulants could have negative effects over time, it helps to first understand what they do in the brain. One hallmark of ADHD is an underactive frontal cortex, a brain region that lies just behind the forehead and controls such "executive" functions as decision making, predicting future events, and suppressing emotions and urges. This area may, in some cases, be smaller than average in ADHD patients, compromising their executive abilities. Frontal cortex function depends greatly on a signaling chemical, or neurotransmitter, called dopamine, which is released in this structure by neurons that originate in deeper brain structures. Less dopamine in the prefrontal cortex is linked, for example, with cognitive difficulty in old age. Another set of dopamine-releasing neurons extends to the [part of the brain known as the] nucleus accumbens, a critical mediator of motivation, pleasure and reward whose function may also be impaired in ADHD.

Stimulants enhance communication in these dopamine-controlled brain circuits by binding to so-called dopamine transporters—the proteins on nerve endings that suck up excess dopamine—thereby deactivating them. As a result, dopamine accumulates outside the neurons, and the additional neurotransmitter is thought to improve the operation of neuronal circuits critical for motivation and impulse control.

Not only can methylphenidate and amphetamine ameliorate a mental deficit, they also can enhance cognitive performance. In studies dating back to the 1970s, researchers have shown that normal children who do not have ADHD also become more attentive—and often calmer—after taking stimulants. In fact, the drugs can lead to higher test scores in students of average and above-average intellectual ability.

Since the 1950s, when doctors first started prescribing stimulants to treat behavior problems, millions of people have taken them without obvious incident. A number of studies have even exonerated them from causing possible adverse effects. For example, researchers have failed to find differences between stimulant-treated children and those not on meds in the larger-scale growth of the brain. In January 2009 child psychiatrist Philip Shaw of the National Institute of Mental Health and his colleagues used MRI [magnetic resonance imaging] scans to measure the change in the thickness of the cerebral cortex (the outer covering of the brain) of 43 youths between the ages of 12 and 16 who had ADHD. The researchers found no evidence that stimulants slowed cortical growth. In fact, only the unmedicated adolescents showed more thinning of the cerebrum than was typical for their age, hinting that the drugs might facilitate normal cortical development in kids with ADHD.

Altering Mood

Despite such positive reports, traces of a sinister side to stimulants have also surfaced. In February 2007 the FDA [US Food and Drug Administration] issued warnings about side effects such as growth stunting and psychosis, among other mental disorders. Indeed, the vast majority of adults with ADHD experience at least one additional psychiatric illness—often an anxiety disorder or drug addiction—in their lifetime. Having ADHD is itself a risk factor for other mental health problems, but the possibility also exists that stimulant treatment during childhood might contribute to these high rates of accompanying diagnoses.

After all, stimulants activate the brain's reward pathways, which are part of the neural circuitry that controls mood under normal conditions. And at least three studies using animals hint that exposure to methylphenidate during childhood may alter mood in the long run, perhaps raising the risk of depression and anxiety in adulthood.

In an experiment published in 2003 psychiatrist Eric Nestler of the University of Texas Southwestern Medical Center and his colleagues injected juvenile rats twice a day with a low dose of methylphenidate similar to that prescribed for children with ADHD. When the rats became adults, the scientists observed the rodents' responses to various emotional stimuli. The rodents that had received methylphenidate were significantly less responsive to natural rewards such as sugar; sex; and fun, novel environments than were untreated rats, suggesting that the drug-exposed animals find such stimuli less pleasurable. In addition, the stimulants apparently made the rats more sensitive to stressful situations such as being forced to swim inside a large tube. Similarly, in the same year psychiatrist William Carlezon of Harvard Medical School and his colleagues reported that methylphenidate-treated preadolescent rats displayed a muted response to a cocaine reward as adults as well as unusual apathy in a forced-swim test, a sign of depression.

In 2008 psychopharmacologist Leandro F. Vendruscolo and his co-workers at Federal University of Santa Catarina in Brazil echoed these results using spontaneously hypertensive rats, which—like children with ADHD—sometimes show attention deficits, hyperactivity and motor impulsiveness. The researchers injected these young rats with methylphenidate for

Long-Term Efficacy of Stimulants Remains Unproven

Long-term efficacy has remained unproven after almost fifty years because the drugs don't work after a few weeks and because they are too hazardous for sufficient numbers of patients to stay on for more than a few weeks at a time.

One of the very few longer-term studies was published in 1997 amid a great deal of media fanfare. It lasted fifteen months and claimed to show a positive effect. However, ten of the original seventy-two children (14 percent) dropped out within one month due to a combination of no drug effect and adverse effects; and of the original participants, approximately one-third completed the study. For these and other reasons, the study has been largely discredited and is seldom mentioned.

Peter R. Breggin, The Ritalin Factbook, *2002.*

16 days at doses approximating those used to treat ADHD in young people. Four weeks later, when the rats were young adults, those that had been exposed to methylphenidate were unusually anxious: they avoided traversing the central area of an open, novel space more so than did rats not exposed to methylphenidate. Adverse effects of this stimulant, the authors speculate, could contribute to the high rates of anxiety disorders among ADHD patients.

Copying Cocaine and Meth?

The long-term use of any drug that affects the brain's reward circuitry also raises the specter of addiction. Methylphenidate has a chemical structure similar to that of cocaine and acts on the brain in a very similar way. Both cocaine and methamphetamine (also called "speed" or "meth")—another highly addictive stimulant—block dopamine transporters just as ADHD drugs do. In the case of the illicit drugs, the dopamine surge is so sudden that in addition to making a person unusually energetic and alert, it produces a "high."

Recent experiments in animals have sounded the alarm that methylphenidate may alter the brain in ways similar to that of more powerfully addictive stimulants such as cocaine. In February 2009 neuroscientists Yong Kim and Paul Greengard, along with their colleagues at the Rockefeller University, reported cocainelike structural and chemical alterations in the brains of mice given methylphenidate. The researchers injected the mice with either methylphenidate or cocaine daily for two weeks. Both treatments increased the density of tiny extensions called spines at the ends of neurons bearing dopamine receptors in the rodent nucleus accumbens. Compared with cocaine, methylphenidate had a somewhat more localized influence; it also had more power over longer spines and less effect on shorter ones. Otherwise, the drugs' effects were strikingly similar.

Furthermore, the scientists found that methylphenidate boosted the amount of a protein called ΔFosB, which turns genes on and off, even more than cocaine did. That result could be a chemical warning of future problems: excess ΔFosB heightens an animal's sensitivity to the rewarding effects of cocaine and makes the animal more likely to ingest the drug. Many former cocaine addicts struggle with depression, anxiety and cognitive problems. Researchers have found that cocaine has remodeled the brains of such ex-users. Similar problems—principally, perhaps, difficulty experiencing joy and excitement in life—could occur after many years of Ritalin or Adderall use.

Amphetamine and methylphenidate can also be addictive if abused by, say, crushing and snorting the pills. In a classic study published in 1995 research psychiatrist Nora Volkow, then at Stony Brook University, and her colleagues showed that injections of methylphenidate produced a cocainelike high in volunteers. More than seven million people in the U.S. have abused methylphenidate, and as many as 750,000 teenagers and young adults show signs of addiction, according to a 2006 report.

Typical oral doses of ADHD meds rarely produce such euphoria and are not usually addicting. Furthermore, the evidence to date, including two 2008 studies from the National Institute on Drug Abuse, indicates that children treated with stimulants early in life are not more likely than other children to become addicted to drugs as adults. In fact, the risk for severe cases of ADHD may run in the opposite direction. (A low addiction risk also jibes with Carlezon's earlier findings, which indicated that methylphenidate use in early life mutes adult rats' response to cocaine.)

Corrupting Cognition

Amphetamines such as Adderall could alter the mind in other ways. A team led by psychologist Stacy A. Castner of the Yale University School of Medicine has documented long-lasting behavioral oddities, such as hallucinations, and cognitive impairment in rhesus monkeys that received escalating injected doses of amphetamine over either six or 12 weeks. Compared with monkeys given inactive saline, the drug-treated monkeys displayed deficits in working memory—the short-term buffer that allows us to hold several items in mind—which persisted for at least three years after exposure to the drug. The researchers connected these cognitive problems to a significantly lower level of dopamine activity in the frontal cortex of the drug-treated monkeys as compared with that of the monkeys not given amphetamine.

Underlying such cognitive and behavioral effects may be subtle structural changes too small to show up on brain scans. In a 1997 study psychologists Terry E. Robinson and Bryan

Kolb of the University of Michigan at Ann Arbor found that high injected doses of amphetamine in rats cause the major output neurons of the nucleus accumbens to sprout longer branches, or dendrites, as well as additional spines on those dendrites. A decade later Castner's team linked lower doses of amphetamine to subtle atrophy of neurons in the prefrontal cortex of monkeys.

A report published in 2005 by neurologist George A. Ricaurte and his team at the Johns Hopkins University School of Medicine is even more damning to ADHD meds because the researchers used realistic doses and drug delivery by mouth instead of by injection. Ricaurte's group trained baboons and squirrel monkeys to self-administer an oral formulation of amphetamine similar to Adderall: the animals drank an amphetamine-laced orange cocktail twice a day for four weeks, mimicking the dosing schedule in humans. Two to four weeks later the researchers detected evidence of amphetamine-induced brain damage, encountering lower levels of dopamine and fewer dopamine transporters on nerve endings in the striatum—a trio of brain regions that includes the nucleus accumbens—in amphetamine-treated primates than in untreated animals. The authors believe these observations reflect a drug-related loss of dopamine-releasing nerve fibers that reach the striatum from the brain stem.

One possible consequence of a loss of dopamine and its associated molecules is Parkinson's disease, a movement disorder that can also lead to cognitive deficits. A study in humans published in 2006 hints at a link between Parkinson's and a prolonged exposure to amphetamine in any form (not just that prescribed for ADHD). Before Parkinson's symptoms such as tremors and muscle rigidity appear, however, dopamine's function in the brain must decline by 80 to 90 percent, or by about twice as much as what Ricaurte and his colleagues saw in baboons that were drinking a more moderate dose of the drug. And some studies have found no connection between stimulant use and Parkinson's.

Stimulants do seem to stunt growth in children. Otherwise, however, studies in humans have largely failed to demonstrate any clear indications of harm from taking ADHD medications as prescribed. Whether the drugs alter the human brain in the same way they alter that of certain animals is unknown, because so far little clinical data exist on their long-term neurological effects. Even when the dosing is similar or the animals have something resembling ADHD, different species' brains may have varying sensitivities to stimulant medications.

Nevertheless, in light of the emerging evidence, many doctors and researchers are recommending a more cautious approach to the medical use of stimulants. Some are urging the adoption of strict diagnostic criteria for ADHD and a policy restricting prescriptions for individuals who fit those criteria. Others are advocating behavior modification—which can be as effective as stimulants over the long run—as a first-line approach to combating the disorder. Certain types of mental exercises may also ease ADHD symptoms. For patients who require stimulants, some neurologists and psychiatrists have also suggested using the lowest dose needed or monitoring the blood levels of these drugs as a way of keeping concentrations below those shown to be problematic in other mammals. Without these or similar measures, large numbers of people who regularly take stimulants may ultimately struggle with a new set of problems spawned by the treatments themselves.

| "ADHD treatments that don't involve
medication have a proven track record."

Nonmedication Treatments for Attention-Deficit/Hyperactivity Disorder Are Effective

Nancy Shute

Nancy Shute is a senior writer at U.S. News & World Report *and instructor in science writing and digital journalism at the Johns Hopkins University in Baltimore. In the following viewpoint, Shute declares that attention-deficit/hyperactivity disorder (ADHD) can be effectively treated without medication. For example, training parents to be clear and specific in their requests and to use rewards and praise instead of punishment is clinically proven to have significant impact on the child, she states. Teaching kids with ADHD life skills in behavioral therapy, Shute contends, can bring social and academic improvements. Also, finding the right treatment—tailored for the individual child—under intensive monitoring is beneficial, she maintains.*

As you read, consider the following questions:

1. What has research determined about changing the behavior of parents of children with ADHD, according to the author?

2. Why are children with ADHD too often prescribed pills, in Shute's view?

3. As stated by Shute, what percentage of children with ADHD do not benefit from medication?

Attention deficit hyperactivity disorder can be a distressing diagnosis, but families have more treatment options than they might realize. Although Ritalin and other stimulant drugs are the most common prescription, ADHD treatments that don't involve medication have a proven track record. And here's a surprise: One of the most beneficial options treats the parents, not the child. For children, skills training programs and ADHD summer camps can help teach techniques to overcome everyday problems that often make life miserable, such as remembering to bring assignments home from school or to listen without interrupting.

Training Parents Helps the Child

Parent skills training has been used for years to improve the behavior of children, and multiple clinical trials have validated its effectiveness. Those same programs improve the behavior of kids with ADHD. Although it may seem odd to be changing parents' behavior to treat what's considered a medical condition in children, research has found that for children with ADHD, having parents who use effective parenting techniques is one of the best predictors of success in adulthood. These programs teach parents to make clear, specific requests of children, for instance, and to use praise and rewards for good behavior far more often than punishment.

In fact, parent training for ADHD is considered so mainstream that last fall [2008] the British government mandated parent training as the first choice for treatment in many cases. "For milder cases, we recommend starting with behavioral therapy," says Eric Taylor, a professor of psychiatry at King's College Hospital and an ADHD authority who helped write the new standards for the National Institute for Health and Clinical Excellence. In England, parents of children with ADHD are offered free government-funded classes where they learn to set clear limits for the child, be consistent in enforcing those limits, and reward good behavior.

Kids All Too Often Just Get Pills

In a perfect world, all children with ADHD would get coordinated, "multimodal" treatment, which would include parent training; a tailored program at school; education about ADHD for kids, parents, and teachers; and medication if necessary. But all too often, kids get just the pills. Most children are treated by pediatricians, who may not be aware of the data on the benefits of behavioral treatments such as parent training, despite the fact that the American Academy of Pediatrics recommends both behavioral interventions and medication. The various professional societies favor their own strengths, not surprisingly, with the psychologists endorsing behavioral therapy and the psychiatrists big on medication as the first line of treatment. "The behavioral treatment had no side effects," says William Pelham, a research psychologist who directs the Center for Children and Families at the University at Buffalo-SUNY [State University of New York] and who was a pioneer in the use of parent training as a behavioral intervention for ADHD. Side effects of medication include insomnia, loss of appetite, and stunted growth. That, he says, is reason enough to follow the British model.

Parents who want to give parent training a try may need to ask around for evidence-based classes. (The National Resource Center on AD/HD is a good place to start, as are community mental health clinics. Ask if the program offered has been validated in clinical trials.) Some popular parenting books are based on clinically validated behavioral treatment. Three good ones: *Parenting the Strong-Willed Child* by Rex Forehand and Nicholas Long, *The Incredible Years* by Carolyn

Webster-Stratton, and *The Kazdin Method for Parenting the Defiant Child* by Alan Kazdin.

"There are some caveats," says Russell Barkley, a clinical psychologist specializing in ADHD treatment and coauthor of the evidence-based parenting manual *Your Defiant Child*. Parent skills training tends to work better for younger children than for teenagers, Barkley says, probably because parents have less influence on teens than they do on 6-year-olds. And in his own research on preschoolers, parent training didn't improve children's behavior at school unless the teacher was also on board. Finally, parent training takes time and effort, because it means not only learning new techniques but also abandoning old habits (adios, nagging).

"Parent training is much more work," Pelham agrees. "It's a pain. But being a parent is a pain."

Teaching Kids Life Skills

It's time to start thinking about new ways to treat ADHD, says Howard Abikoff, director of the Institute for Attention Deficit Hyperactivity and Behavior Disorders at the New York University Child Study Center. "Do we have enough evidence-based treatments to say we know how to deal with the problems in these folks' lives?" he asks. "I don't think so."

Many children with ADHD struggle with social skills, such as waiting for their turn to talk instead of interrupting or keeping their temper instead of dissing teachers. Increasingly, programs are trying to solve that problem with behavioral treatments that offer rigorously tested skills training. Duke University Medical Center's ADHD program, for one, offers classes for third to fifth graders on listening and following directions, homework, organizational skills, effective communication, and problem-solving. ADHD therapeutic summer programs, including the Summer Treatment Programs founded by Pelham, as well as ADHD summer camps offer skills training at a level that might not be available closer to home. Mary

Alvord, a clinical psychologist in Rockville, Md., offers weekly group sessions using cognitive behavioral therapy to help children with ADHD improve their social skills. "We also mix in kids with social anxiety," Alvord says. "They provide excellent modeling opportunities and support for one another."

Abikoff is halfway through a National Institute of Mental Health–funded clinical trial to test whether children with ADHD can be taught to become better at organizing, time management, and planning, three skills that many continue to struggle with as working adults. "If you've ever looked in the book bag of some of these children, it's quite remarkable," Abikoff says. "Even if the kids are doing everything in the classroom that we've worked on with them, it's still possible that they'll come home and they don't have it," Abikoff says. "We try to provide them with reminders at the point where it's critical to remember—something attached to the zipper of their book bag. It's the last thing they do before they walk out."

Finding the Right Treatment

Scientists now know that ADHD takes different forms, and those differences are probably rooted in brain physiology. For instance, about 20 percent of children get no benefit from stimulant medications, but right now the only way to find out who does is by trying the drugs. Someday there may be a simple test that will tell parents just what form of ADHD their child has and what treatment will work best. For now, alas, finding the right fit is all too often lots of trial, too much error. Just one example: Doctors and therapists often recommend "talk" or "play" therapy for the child, even though there is no evidence that it helps with ADHD. Indeed, behavioral treatments that teach skills to parents or children are the only nonmedical form of ADHD therapy with solid scientific evidence that they work.

Training Teachers to Handle ADHD Pupils

Training teachers and other school personnel in interventions and accommodations and helping them gain more knowledge of ADHD are critical in the implementation of multimodal treatment. Teachers who do not understand the nature of ADHD and grasp the need for treatment are less likely to effectively implement interventions. Teachers have consistently expressed a desire for training in effective interventions for students with ADHD and lack of training is perceived as a significant barrier to working effectively with students with ADHD. Lack of training is a particularly serious problem among general education teachers. General education teachers will typically have a child with ADHD for most of the school day, yet often they have not received systematic instruction in skills critical to working with students with ADHD, such as behavior management techniques, in the course of their teacher training programs. They may also lack knowledge of medication management, effective accommodations, working with parents, and psychological support. Need for training is critical because there is evidence that insufficiently trained teachers may implement interventions incorrectly or in a manner that renders the intervention ineffective. General education teachers may also be more resistant to implement some interventions, especially those that involve altering instruction.

Robert Reid and Joseph Johnson,
Teacher's Guide to ADHD, 2012.

In the 1990s, the National Institute of Mental Health tried to weigh the relative benefits of the two most common treatments for ADHD: stimulant drugs and behavioral treatments, including parent training. The Multimodal Treatment Study of Children with ADHD followed 579 grade-schoolers for 14 months. Some got stimulants, and some got behavioral therapy that included parent training, teacher training, and a summer camp that taught the kids social skills. A third group got both medication and the behavioral intervention. A fourth group had treatments chosen by their parents in the community. At the end, the children in all four groups were doing better. Parents and teachers rated the medication-only group as having many fewer symptoms of inattention and hyperactivity/ impulsivity. But they rated the children who got behavioral treatment as doing better on aggressive behavior, peer relations, parent-child relations, and academic achievement. Since the first results were published in 1999, researchers have been arguing strenuously over whether the study proves that medication or treatment without medication is best.

"What the MTA really showed is that it's not the medication per se but the intensive monitoring," says Benedetto Vitiello, chief of the child and adolescent treatment and preventive interventions branch for the National Institute of Mental Health. "Having a visit each month, putting together all the information for the school and the parent, tailoring the treatment." Indeed, when the study ended and the extra monitoring stopped, the benefits faded for all groups, medicated or not.

The take-home message for parents: There are other good treatments besides the pills, but no treatment's going to work without sustained effort from the whole family.

| *"Cannabis should be considered first in the treatment of post-traumatic stress disorder."*

Medical Marijuana Should Be Considered as a Treatment for Post-Traumatic Stress Disorder

Steve Fox

Steve Fox is the director of government relations at the Marijuana Policy Project and coauthor of Marijuana Is Safer: So Why Are We Driving People to Drink? *In the following viewpoint, Fox contends that medical marijuana must be considered as a treatment for post-traumatic stress disorder (PTSD) to help the nation's veterans. Research shows that antidepressants and antipsychotics are no more effective than placebos in treating the disorder, he contends. In addition, evidence supports the potential of medical marijuana as a treatment for PTSD and its safety as a therapeutically active substance, Fox states. But antidrug forces in the federal government and marijuana's classification as a Schedule I drug prevent researchers from performing clinical studies, he asserts, delaying relief for suffering veterans.*

As you read, consider the following questions:

1. As described by Fox, what did Irit Akirav discover about the potential benefits of marijuana for patients with PTSD?

2. How is research on medical marijuana for PTSD stymied, according to the author?

3. Why is federal marijuana policy illogical, in Fox's view?

Antidepressants or antipsychotic medications are among the most common medications [used] to treat post-traumatic stress disorder and the insomnia, anger, nightmares and anxiety that often come with it.

Unfortunately, they're not guaranteed to be much help.

That's what a study in August's [2011] *Journal of the American Medical Association* suggested. Risperdal, a widely prescribed antipsychotic, is no more effective in treating PTSD than placebos, it reported. This finding adds to earlier research on the ineffectiveness of most PTSD medications.

Marijuana Needs Further Research

But there is a drug that has been shown to alleviate the symptoms of PTSD. Unfortunately, Veterans Affairs doctors can't recommend it, and the federal government won't allow research to proceed that could prove its effectiveness. What's the drug? Marijuana.

Sixteen states and the District of Columbia have medical marijuana laws on the books, but we are still a long way from general acceptance of the drug as a medicine. If we're serious about seeking an effective remedy for post-traumatic stress, and serving the hundreds of thousands of veterans with the disorder, this needs to change. It's not a guaranteed solution, but sufficient evidence exists to show that it's a treatment that needs to be explored further.

In 2006, one of the pioneers of medical marijuana in the United States, the late Tod Mikuriya, published a paper in a cannabis research journal reporting on his experience with PTSD sufferers. He compared marijuana to commonly prescribed medications and noted that the former worked better to control chronic stressors, without adverse side effects. "Based on both safety and efficacy," he wrote, "cannabis should be considered first in the treatment of post-traumatic stress disorder."

A few years later, the Israeli physician Irit Akirav published a study in the *Journal of Neuroscience* that alluded to the potential benefits of marijuana for PTSD patients. He found in an animal study that cannabinoids—the active chemicals in marijuana—may reduce the effects of PTSD. "The results of our research," Akirav noted, "should encourage psychiatric investigation into using cannabinoids in post-traumatic stress patients."

In New Mexico, where PTSD was added as a qualifying condition to the state's medical marijuana program after an evaluation of the available research, more patients use marijuana for PTSD than for any other condition.

Veterans, if given the option to use marijuana to alleviate PTSD, would probably take advantage of the opportunity. In September [2011], the military newspaper *Stars and Stripes* published a story about Army Sgt. Jamey Raines, who talked openly about how he had used marijuana to treat PTSD triggered by heavy combat duty in Iraq. Marijuana was not just helpful, Raines said—it was the only substance he found effective.

A Victim of Marijuana Politics

Of course this evidence is still limited and in some cases anecdotal; for conclusive answers, we need FDA [US Food and Drug Administration]-approved research to assess the benefits of marijuana in a clinical environment. Fortunately, earlier this year [2011], the FDA approved such a protocol to study the therapeutic potential of marijuana for veterans suffering from chronic, treatment-resistant PTSD. But that's where the good news ends.

If this were any other drug, the researchers would probably be organizing or conducting trials now. But this isn't a new chemical compound dreamed up by a pharmaceutical company. It's marijuana, and the anti-marijuana forces in the federal government are powerful.

Here is how this research has been stymied. In April [2011], the researchers submitted their protocol to the Public Health Service (PHS) and the National Institute on Drug Abuse (NIDA) along with a request to purchase marijuana from NIDA, which has a monopoly on the supply of pot used for research in the United States. In September, the PHS and NIDA rejected the protocol and refused the researchers' request to purchase marijuana for the study. They criticized the protocol design—the same design that the FDA had approved—and directed the researchers to redesign it and resubmit it, a process that will result in at least an additional year's delay. The reviewers even reserved the right to raise new criticisms after the old ones had been addressed. It is likely that the researchers will never be able to purchase the marijuana from NIDA.

The research, it seems, is a victim of marijuana politics. Under federal law, a drug is considered most harmful—and placed in the most restrictive category, Schedule I—if it has "no currently accepted medical use." Although marijuana was listed as a medicine in the U.S. Pharmacopoeia before its prohibition and was widely used for dozens of conditions, Congress temporarily placed it in Schedule I in 1970, pending the outcome of a government study. The study, produced by a national commission on drug abuse, ultimately concluded that marijuana's harmful effects were so limited for light and moderate users that it should not even be a criminal offense to use it. But its status as a Schedule I drug has not changed.

Ignoring Marijuana's Therapeutic Value

Advocates have been working toward a change since 1972, when the first petition to reschedule marijuana was filed with the Bureau of Narcotics and Dangerous Drugs, the predecessor of the Drug Enforcement Administration [DEA]. After many refusals to act and a few court rulings, the DEA finally initiated hearings on rescheduling in 1986—14 years after the first filing.

These hearings led to an opinion in 1988 by the DEA's chief administrative law judge, Francis Young, who wrote: "Marijuana, in its natural form, is one of the safest therapeutically active substances known to man. . . . It would be unreasonable, arbitrary and capricious for DEA to continue to stand between those sufferers and the benefits of this substance in light of the evidence in this record." He concluded that the provisions of the Controlled Substances Act "permit and require" the transfer of marijuana from Schedule I to a less restrictive category.

Yet the DEA administrator did not reclassify marijuana. Since that time, the agency has denied two other rescheduling petitions, most recently in July [2011].

It is bad enough that the DEA has repeatedly ignored existing evidence regarding marijuana's therapeutic value in order to maintain the drug's Schedule I status. But both the DEA and NIDA have taken further steps to block any new evidence from being produced. Most notably, the DEA has refused for 10 years to grant a license to the University of Massachusetts to cultivate marijuana for FDA-approved research, providing a privately funded alternative source to NIDA's marijuana supply. The refusal has occurred despite yet another DEA administrative law judge ruling that the license would be "in the public interest" and should be granted.

Trapped in Absurd Circular Logic

Federal marijuana policy is thus trapped in absurd circular logic. Officials argue that marijuana must be kept illegal because it is a "dangerous" Schedule I drug. They refuse to move it out of Schedule I, claiming that there is no evidence that it has medical value. They refuse to allow private entities to cultivate marijuana for research to demonstrate that it has medical value. And they set up endless obstacles for any researchers who hope to conduct potentially favorable studies with the marijuana controlled by the government. No research, no evidence, no rescheduling. Therefore, marijuana is still dangerous.

The federal government's stance has led to our current state-by-state battles over medical marijuana. We will continue to fight and will add more states to the pro-medical-marijuana side of the ledger. But it will be many years, possibly decades, before marijuana is legal for medical purposes in all 50 states.

When current and former service men and women are seriously suffering—to the point where some have even taken their own lives—we at least owe it to them to explore any treatment that might be effective.

It is time for government officials to take this nation's veterans off the medical marijuana battlefield. NIDA should grant the researchers' request to purchase marijuana and allow the FDA-approved PTSD study of veterans to move forward. These brave men and women don't have decades to wait for relief.

> "The medical community remains divided on whether marijuana should be used to treat PTSD."

Some Experts Disagree That Medical Marijuana Should Be Considered as a Treatment for Post-Traumatic Stress Disorder

Joey Peters

In the following viewpoint, Joey Peters observes why some experts oppose medical marijuana to treat post-traumatic stress disorder (PTSD). Peters explains that in New Mexico—one of three states that approve it for the disorder—a physician petitioned to remove PTSD from the medical cannabis program on several grounds: It exposed PTSD patients to an addictive substance, marijuana is not supported by clinical studies to treat the disorder, and patients may form a dependence on it rather than seek long-term treatment. Nonetheless, Peters points out, the petition was met with resistance by other experts with anecdotal evidence of the drug's effectiveness. The author is a staff writer for the Santa Fe Reporter *in New Mexico.*

As you read, consider the following questions:

1. According to the author, what does William Ulwilling argue about New Mexico's offering medical marijuana to sufferers of PTSD?

2. Why did researchers at the University of Arizona find little evidence supporting medical marijuana as an effective treatment for PTSD, as reported by Peters?

3. What is David Bennahum's opinion of treating PTSD with medical marijuana, as cited by the author?

On July 27 [2012], Dr. William Ulwelling, an Albuquerque psychiatrist for more than 30 years, wrote a letter to the head of the state's medical marijuana program that may have large implications for nearly half of the program's patients.

"At the next hearing of the Medical Cannabis Advisory Board [MCAB]," he wrote, "I will petition the removal of Posttraumatic Stress Disorder [PTSD] from the list of eligible medical conditions for enrollment in the NM Medical Cannabis Program [MCP]."

New Mexico is one of only three states with programs that recognize medical marijuana as a legitimate treatment for PTSD. PTSD sufferers make up the bulk of the MCP's patients, at roughly 40 percent. Many of them are veterans.

For the next two and a half months, the petition remained largely under the radar, but rumors swelled throughout the medical marijuana community. Last week [in October 2012], it finally went public, and medical marijuana advocates across the state responded with a backlash.

"It's insane. It's ridiculous," Len Goodman, executive director of medical marijuana producer New MexiCann Natural Medicine, tells SFR [*Santa Fe Reporter*]. "Sure, it's not for everybody. But for those who think they should use cannabis, why in the world would you want to turn them into criminals?"

Ulwelling says his concern stems from exposing PTSD patients to an "addictive substance"—marijuana—for a treatment that isn't backed up by sufficient clinical evidence. (Studies on the addictive properties of marijuana have been largely conflicting, however.)

"They're probably dependent on this stuff," Ulwelling told medical marijuana advocate Larry Love recently on Love's Medical Marijuana Radio podcast. "I would ask, 'What the heck is the state of New Mexico [doing,] making medical opinions against the overwhelming consensus of experts in the field?' I would stress that my opinion is not some nutcase opinion—it is the overwhelming consensus opinion of experts in the field."

But Love pointed out that Ulwelling's petition could harm the nearly 3,000 PTSD patients across the state.

"As a man—as a human being—how will you feel, knowing that your actions will cause so much pain to already-suffering people, especially the veterans of our wars?" Love asked.

Similarly, nurse practitioner Bryan Krumm, who manages patients enrolled in the program, is threatening to file a formal complaint against Ulwelling if he doesn't rescind the petition. In an Oct. 3 letter to Ulwelling, Krumm accused him of attempting to use his medical license "to do harm to thousands of New Mexico citizens."

"I will not allow such gross misconduct to go unchallenged," Krumm wrote. "I can only assume now that your position is based on arrogance, ignorance and/or intolerance. Medicine must be based on science, not politics."

Research Is Limited and Anecdotal

But medical research on the subject—some of which suggests that marijuana can help alleviate PTSD symptoms—is still limited and largely anecdotal.

In June [2012], for instance, researchers at the University of Arizona found little evidence supporting marijuana as either an effective or ineffective treatment for PTSD. That's largely due to marijuana's federal classification as a Schedule I controlled substance—meaning it's illegal and viewed as having no medicinal value—which has prevented adequate research on the subject.

The medical community remains divided on whether marijuana should be used to treat PTSD. Carola Kieve, a psychiatrist at the Community Mental Health Center in rural northern New Mexico, says she's seen two of her patients with PTSD drop their addictions to harmful drugs after enrolling in the cannabis program.

"The availability of treatment, for any diagnosis in this area, is scarce," she writes in an email to SFR. "I see absolutely no harm with [medical marijuana's] use in patients with PTSD."

Attesting to Pot's Benefits

Like Kieve's patients, many PTSD sufferers attest to cannabis' benefits, and several hundred are planning to show up during Ulwelling's appearance before the MCAB on Nov. 7. [His petition was rejected.]

One of them is Santa Fe resident Nat Dean, who suffered severe injuries in a car wreck in 1984. A few years ago, she was diagnosed with PTSD. Dean, who also suffers from chronic pain, says her symptoms spiked after pancreatitis forced her to have her bladder removed. She says that bad health care experiences were "the icing on the cake" for her PTSD symptoms.

"I feel like, [with] everything that was going wrong for me, I wasn't able to handle everyday living," Dean tells SFR. "You think you're losing your mind."

Marijuana as a Treatment for PTSD

The studies with the highest quality ratings generally find an association between PTSD and marijuana use but the study designs do not allow for determination [regarding whether] one causes or aggravates the other, or if both are associated with some unknown third factor. We could not find any research that directly addressed the key questions of the benefits and harms of marijuana use for treatment of PTSD. The most relevant literature generally was of low or very low quality and no conclusions can be drawn about the benefits or harms of marijuana use for the treatment of PTSD.

Doug Campos-Outcalt,
Patricia Hamilton, and Cecilia Rosales,
Medical Marijuana for the Treatment
of Post Traumatic Stress Disorder, *2012.*

At one point, Dean was on 27 different drugs. Now, that number is down to six, and Dean largely credits cannabis for her recovery. She smokes two or three puffs of marijuana at night every few days.

Ulwelling concedes that patients like Dean may benefit from medical marijuana, but he argues that allowing the program to continue offering it to PTSD sufferers without proper scientific evidence could cause more harm than good.

He worries that some PTSD sufferers may come to rely on pot indefinitely, rather than seeking proper, long-term treatment.

"Marijuana can make you feel good," Ulwelling tells SFR, adding that beer can, too. "Just because people say, 'I've been helped by this' [doesn't mean] that's the end of it."

He adds that if his petition is successful, current PTSD-suffering medical marijuana patients in New Mexico should probably be "grandfathered in" since they, in good faith, relied on the state to admit them to the MCP.

Ulwelling's Priorities Questioned

Medical marijuana advocates question Ulwelling's priorities, noting that he hasn't treated a patient in five years, and that a 2007 lawsuit blamed him for a patient's suicide. However, the court ruled that Ulwelling committed no wrongdoing, and such lawsuits are also common for physicians like Ulwelling—a recent *New England Journal of Medicine* study concluded that at least 75 percent of physicians will be sued at least once in the course of their careers.

The University of New Mexico [UNM] also took issue with Ulwelling's signature on the petition, in which he identified himself as a "clinical assistant professor" at UNM's medical school. UNM says Ulwelling hasn't had a contract there for five years.

Ulwelling says he started as a clinical assistant professor with the school in 1984 and that his contract could have become inactive since his semi-retirement a few years ago. He adds that his petition is in no way meant to represent UNM, and that he's in contact with the university and will change his signature to "former clinical assistant professor" if instructed to do so.

In his debate with Ulwelling, Love mentioned that research on the issue was still developing, and cited recent studies in Israel showing benefits.

"You need more research before you can take this medicine away from people," Love told Ulwelling on his podcast.

But Ulwelling argues just the opposite—that more research needs to be done before PTSD sufferers should be allowed to take marijuana.

"In a sense, we're doing that experiment now—on the citizens of New Mexico," he says.

To others in the medical industry, the dispute as to whether PTSD should be treated with marijuana is a low priority. David Bennahum, a UNM School of Medicine professor and a member of the school's Institute for Ethics, recently told SFR that the issue is a distraction from larger problems such as a lack of holistic health care.

"Today, we're very focused on pharmacology," he said. "It's much cheaper for insurance providers to pay for drugs than psychotherapy. It's not surprising, in a society that uses so many drugs, that we turn to drugs for our problems, because we're not invested in therapy."

▌ *"Key to success is CBT treatment."*

Cognitive Behavioral Therapy Is an Effective Treatment for Obsessive-Compulsive Disorder

Allen Weg

Allen Weg is a psychologist, the vice president of the New Jersey Obsessive-Compulsive Foundation, and the author of OCD and Storytelling: The Use of Metaphor in Treatment. *In the following viewpoint, he maintains that obsessive-compulsive disorder (OCD) can be effectively managed with cognitive behavioral therapy (CBT), specifically with exposure and response prevention (ERP). Unlike talk therapy, the author claims, CBT focuses on the present rather than on the past or on subconscious processes, and ERP works to gradually desensitize patients to the obsessions, anxieties, and other triggers of repetitive behaviors. CBT can also be combined with medication in some cases, but successful treatment depends on finding a therapist that specializes in CBT and its protocols.*

As you read, consider the following questions:

1. What happens in an "exposure trial" in ERP, as described by Weg?

2. According to Weg, what does CBT achieve for parents and their children?

3. When should a patient (or the parent of a minor patient) move on to another therapist, in the author's opinion?

When clients come to a cognitive behavioral therapist with an anxiety disorder, such as obsessive-compulsive disorder, the focus of the therapy is an intervention called "exposure and response prevention," or ERP. It means just what it sounds like—a person repeatedly approaches or is "exposed to" the very thing that makes him or her anxious or uncomfortable, and then attempts to stop themselves from engaging in behaviors that are designed to lower that anxiety.

Cognitive behavioral therapy (CBT), in contrast to traditional "talk" therapy, is shorter in duration and focuses not so much on early life experiences or unconscious processes, but rather on "here and now" problems, and on the education and coaching of clients as they learn new ways to think and behave in order to solve those problems.

In OCD, obsessions, or anxiety-producing intrusive thoughts or images, are usually followed by compulsions, or behaviors that the person does on purpose to lower that anxiety. For instance, if an obsession takes the form of "that thing is dirty/contaminated" the compulsion would be to avoid touching that thing, or to wash excessively if you did touch it. ERP would then involve the person touching "contaminated" things on purpose, followed by specific efforts on the part of the person to NOT wash.

In ERP, with repeated and lengthy "exposure trials," the person "learns" to let go of these fears through a process called "desensitization." Essentially, after exposing themselves repeatedly to a feared thought, thing or situation over and over again, they get used to it, and it bothers them less and less over time.

Because this is initially a very scary process, clients with OCD do these exposures as slowly or as fast as they feel they can handle, thereby allowing them to feel in control of the therapy. In addition, ERP is usually done one small step at a time, so that clients can "build up their strength" much like one would do by lifting weights, starting with lighter weights first and then "graduating" to heavier and heavier weights as they build their strength.

This metaphor of weight lifting is just one of the many stories that I use when conducting therapy. To help clients and their families understand ERP, which at first can sound very scary and quite strange, I use different stories to help them understand how this process works.

Using Metaphor for Understanding

Storytelling and metaphor use is often the best way to present subtle and confusing ideas in a succinct and concrete way. It is a wonderful way to go beyond merely describing something or even explaining it. Narratives serve to illustrate not just an idea, but the very foundation of an idea. By hearing a story, the listener shares an experience with the narrator which enables him to understand what is being discussed in a way that mere description cannot accomplish. It is a way to get inside the mind of the narrator.

OCD is relatively simple and easy to describe, but it is extremely difficult to fully understand. Once presented with information about this psychiatric disorder, we are left with the questions, "OK, I get what happens, but how can that be? How does that make sense? Why are people thinking and doing those crazy things?"

As strange as OCD symptoms are, they don't hold a candle to the treatment. The cognitive behavioral treatment of OCD involves some of the most bizarre and outrageous interventions that you are ever likely to encounter in a therapy office. Most OCD clients are very surprised or even stunned when it is explained to them what they need to do in order to help make themselves better. They sometimes think the therapist is crazier than they feel.

And so something beyond telling is required. Explanations don't seem sufficient when you are being instructed to think and behave in a way that seems contradictory to your goals. It is often hard to "think outside the box," to think nonlinearly.

In the arts, whether we are referring to dance, music, sculpture, painting, writing, poetry, theater, or film making, there are countless examples of an emotion, a struggle, or an experience of some kind, which is communicated indirectly and expressed through the artistic medium. This artistic representation, when done effectively, allows the audience to better understand what is being communicated than if the idea being presented was done so by mere instruction. And so it is with describing the diagnosis and the treatment of OCD.

In terms of children and OCD, parents might not be sure when they should begin to worry. Children, especially younger children, tend to be superstitious, magical in their thinking, and compulsive and repetitive in their behaviors.

They may demand to be told the same bedtime stories night after night, insist that they line up their stuffed animals in a particular order, have a meltdown if the peas touch the mashed potatoes on their dinner plate, and play games such as "step on a crack break your mother's back." These are all healthy attempts to feel a little more in control of one's life when you are a little person living in a world completely dominated by grownups.

But when these rituals become non-functional and non-flexible, when they cause undue and chronic distress to the child as well as the family, then parents might need to consider professional intervention. No one instance or behavior alone may constitute the diagnosis, but if the child is completely unable to control his or her behavior, and is completely inflexible about altering it, and the behavior is excessive to the point of significantly interfering with functioning, whether at school, at home, or during a specific activity such as bathing, eating or getting ready for bed, then that is the time to seek professional help.

Finding the Right Therapist

The good news is that help is available, and that we in the mental health field have gotten pretty good at helping most people with OCD to a significant degree. We don't have what one would call a cure (yet), but rather we teach children how to manage their OCD, and help parents help their kids to achieve the same goal. They may even get to the point where they seem to have no symptoms, even for a long time, but chances are that the OCD will re-emerge at a later time, especially when the child is stressed due to illness, lack of sleep, or a life change such as a move of residence or the death of a loved one, including a pet.

Treatment for many children usually consists of a combination of medication and cognitive behavioral therapy. Typically, these medicines fall in the class of SSRIs (Selective Seretonin Reuptake Inhibitors), but other medications are used as well, or instead of these, especially if there has not been a therapeutic response to the initial medication trials. Many children are able to utilize therapy without the addition of medication.

Key to success is CBT treatment. But finding a good therapist may not be easy. You want someone who identifies themselves as a CBT therapist, and one that uses ERP as a treatment protocol. Interview your prospective therapist. Ask how many OCD children they have worked with, and how they treated them. If you don't hear ERP and CBT in the answer, or if you hear things like"relaxation training," move onto someone else.

The first stop to finding a good therapist is the national OC Foundation, which has a Web site at www.ocfoundation-.org. They have a referral list for the whole country. Most established therapists have a Web site these days, and it is a good thing to check them out and see what they have to say about the clinician.

If your child has OCD—no matter that the symptoms are severe or that it has been going on for a long time—there is a good chance that they, and you, will get significant relief from treatment, and in a relatively short period of time (weeks, not months), especially if they have never been treated before, or have never had CBT treatment before. There is every reason to be extremely hopeful. The key is to find the right therapist, and psychiatrist, if medication is needed.

There are also some Intensive Outpatient Programs (IOPs) across the country, and a small handful of inpatient hospitals that cater specifically to OCD, though many do not treat children. Again, the www.OCFoundation.org provides information on these resources as well.

Finally, if your child has had a very severe and acute onset of OCD symptoms, and especially if this was preceded by a strep infection, there is the chance that your child has type of OCD triggered by an autoimmune illness. This type of OCD is treated with antibiotics as well as CBT. Check with your physician first.

Periodical and Internet Sources Bibliography

The following articles have been selected to supplement the diverse views presented in this chapter.

Jeff Brady	"Can Marijuana Ease PTSD? A Debate Brews," National Public Radio, May 19, 2010. www.npr.org.
Jeffrey Kluger	"A Better Way to Treat Obsessive-Compulsive Kids," *Time*, September 26, 2011.
Harold Koplewicz	"Why 'Ritalin Gone Wrong' Is Wrong," *Huffington Post*, January 31, 2012. www.huffingtonpost.com.
Randy LoBasso	"Iraq War Veterans Turn to Marijuana for Managing PTSD Symptoms," *Philadelphia Weekly*, January 25, 2012.
Martin Mulcahey	"The Case for Treating PTSD in Veterans with Medical Marijuana," *Atlantic Monthly*, January 17, 2012.
Frederic Neuman	"Why Is OCD So Hard to Treat?," Fighting Fear Blog, *Psychology Today*, July 12, 2012. www.psychologytoday.com.
Kimberly Quinan	"OCD & Anxiety: Five Common Roadblocks to Successful Treatment," OCD Center of Los Angeles Blog, July 12, 2012. www.ocdla.com.
L. Alan Sroufe	"Ritalin Gone Wrong," *New York Times*, January 28, 2012.
Wall Street Journal	"Are ADHD Medications Overprescribed?," September 14, 2012.
Emily Willingham	"Should Children Take ADHD Drugs—Even If They Don't Have the Disorder?," *Forbes*, October 9, 2012.

CHAPTER 4

What Policies Will Best Address the Challenges of Behavioral Disorders?

Chapter Preface

In 1988, the National Vaccine Injury Compensation Program (VICP) established what is known as the "vaccine court," which aims to award individuals who suffer from the adverse effects of vaccines. "The VICP compensates people whom a federal court determines to have met legal standards for having been injured by vaccines; these standards do not need to meet the standards of scientific causation," states the National Network for Immunization Information. The program is also intended to protect vaccine supplies and control their costs. To file a claim in vaccine court, the petitioner is not required to show proof of negligence against the health care provider or manufacturer; however, to qualify for compensation, the petitioner must demonstrate that the injury (defined by the Vaccine Injury Table) occurred within a prescribed time period of receiving the vaccine, the vaccine caused the injury, or the vaccine worsened a preexisting condition. Money awarded in claims is funded by a vaccine tax.

When a number of petitioners began to file claims in 2001 alleging that the vaccine for measles, mumps, and rubella that contained the mercury-based preservative thimerosal had caused autism in their children, the Omnibus Autism Proceeding was created to arbitrate these cases. As of May 2012, a total of $2.44 billion had been awarded to thousands of families and individuals under the VICP. "The vaccine marketplace remains healthy; liability-related vaccine shortages a distant memory, new vaccines are being licensed, and many are in various stages of development," state Katherine M. Cook and Geoffrey Evans of the Division of Vaccine Injury Compensation, US Department of Health and Human Services. Cook and Evans add that "the VICP continues to fulfill the intent of Congress by providing an accessible and efficient alternative for people found to be injured by certain childhood vaccines."

But opponents argue that the VICP is a failure. "Almost four out of five claimants lose in what was meant to be a petitioner-friendly administrative forum," contend Mary Holland and Robert Krakow, legal experts who specialize in autism and vaccines. "The tenor of VICP proceedings is exceptionally hostile and adversarial—the exact opposite of what Congress intended. Petitioners must litigate almost every case—almost no injuries are 'on-table' administrative claims anymore." Furthermore, Holland and Krakow assert that the vaccine court lacks the judicial integrity to arbitrate vaccine injury claims, which could influence future laws. "Decisions in cases like the Omnibus Autism Proceeding potentially affect national vaccination policy. [The vaccine court], lacking the life tenure of judges or even long-term appointments, [is] not suited to make decisions that might affect federal policy," they claim.

Experts, as well, offer conflicting views on the causes of autism and other behavioral disorders, which can make policy decisions difficult for public officials and professionals. The viewpoints in the following chapter examine policies that address the evaluation and treatment of autism in school-age children and personality and post-traumatic stress disorders in veterans.

> *"A big factor for [autistic students'] future success, say the experts, is being educated in regular classes, where they can learn to interact with their peers and to control or modify their behaviors."*

Mainstreaming Benefits Autistic Students

Cindy Long

Cindy Long is a senior writer and editor for NEA Today, *the magazine of the National Education Association. In the following viewpoint, Long argues that enrolling autistic students in regular classes can teach them to engage with others and manage their behaviors, which will help them to lead independent and productive lives. Inclusion programs, she contends, not only assist them in the transition from special education, they demonstrate that autistic students are capable of academic achievement, excel in certain subjects, and have unique cognitive skills. Moreover, mainstreaming imparts respect and tolerance to all students, Long maintains.*

Cindy Long, "Going Mainstream: Early Intervention and Inclusion Open Doors for Children with Autism," *NEA Today*, vol. 26, no. 5, February 2008, p. 37. Copyright © 2008 by NEA Today. All rights reserved. Reproduced by permission.

As you read, consider the following questions:

1. What fear is a roadblock for general education teachers to teach autistic students, in the author's opinion?

2. According to Long, how does Kristen, an autistic student, perform better than regular students?

3. How do regular students treat and view Nick, an autistic student, according to the author?

Halfway though the morning lesson, 7-year-old Dan starts screeching, pressing his hands tightly over his ears and rocking violently forward and back in his chair. Some students don't seem to notice, but it's sensory overload for others, who get distracted or simply shut down. They're in a special education classroom for autistic children at Henry B. Milnes School in Fair Lawn, New Jersey, but despite their developmental and behavioral challenges, many of them, including Dan, will eventually be "mainstreamed," spending part or even most of the school day in general education classrooms.

It's estimated that one in 150 children in the United States have autism. There's no cure, but with early diagnosis and the hard work of dedicated educators, many autistic kids will grow up to live independently, and even make extraordinary contributions to society. A big factor for their future success, say the experts, is being educated in regular classes, where they can learn to interact with their peers and to control or modify their behaviors.

The "Fear Factor"

But transitions are difficult for children with autism, and sometimes inclusion is tough on teachers, too. No matter how great their desire to help, some teachers see a student like Dan and fear they won't be able to handle teaching an autistic child alongside the rest of their students. That "fear factor" is a big roadblock for general education teachers, says Julie

Moore, a middle school teacher and member of NEA's [National Education Association] IDEA Resource Cadre.

Moore spent much of the last two decades teaching in special ed classrooms. When the inclusion movement took hold, she saw nervous and unprepared general education teachers in need of support. That's when she began leading a six-hour autism workshop for Washington teachers based on *The Puzzle of Autism*, a resource guide created by NEA and the Autism Society of America.

"The best advice is to keep a sense of humor and don't be afraid to try new things," says Moore. "And, of course, the paraprofessionals are always there to assist you. Once a child is mainstreamed, we don't cut the supports."

She says successful inclusion programs prepare everyone for the transition—not only the autistic child, but also the educators. And the process begins long before the child flies from the special education nest.

Mainstreaming Kristen

Nancy Potter is a paraprofessional who has worked with an autistic 9-year-old named Kristen since she was in first grade. Kristen trusts her completely (although she went through a phase when she couldn't tolerate Potter wearing brown). Like most paraprofessionals who work with students with disabilities, Potter sits beside Kristen in class, ready to assist her, quiet her, or remove her from the class when her behavior becomes a distraction.

Kristen has long blonde hair, a sharp sense of humor, and a strong aversion to geese or pelicans, though she no longer screams when entering a McDonald's. She speaks louder than most people, in a husky monotone, but she has a ready smile and now looks people in the eye without hesitation. She spends most of each day in the general education class with the other fourth-graders at the Milnes School.

"I was a little nervous about it at first," admits Kristen's teacher, Carol Granoff. "I thought there'd be a lot of screaming, but it's more like fretting. And if she has a problem, she simply returns to the special education classroom. But she's just amazing, and she grasps so much. She gets 100s on most of her tests, and she has such a memory."

To prepare for Kristen's arrival, Granoff talked to the special education teachers and paraprofessionals who had worked with her over the years, as well as her third-grade teacher, who offered a lot of practical advice.

Granoff learned that she should give Kristen more time to complete assignments, and allow her to work on projects more independently and creatively. While the rest of the class discussed healthy breakfast options in a health education unit, for example, Kristen colored a food pyramid worksheet.

Like many children with autism, Kristen excels in specific subjects (spelling is her favorite) and has unusual cognitive abilities. Granoff regularly assigns spelling words to the class and then reads them aloud the next day, using a particular pattern to reorder the words before asking the students to spell them. She soon found that Kristen could decipher the pattern. "She'd have the next word spelled before I even said it," says Granoff.

Other classroom activities challenge Kristen. When Granoff dims the lights and shows a video, Kristen gets agitated and needs to leave the room. "But whenever there's a problem, Nancy's there to support her and ease her back into the lesson, or to take her out of the room," Granoff says.

Working with Dan in Special Ed

Back in the special education classroom down the hall, a paraprofessional works to bring Dan back into the lesson. To quiet his screeching, she asks him to push a button on his "Hip Talk," a small device resembling a fanny pack with icons of faces expressing different emotions, like sad, angry, and scared. Dan pushes a button and a recorded voice says, "I'm angry."

"He's angry because he wants to draw," explains special education teacher Jennifer Gruber. "A lot of problem behaviors we see in kids with autism result from their inability to express themselves. Hip Talk allows Dan to tell us what he's feeling."

Dan's screams have quieted, but he continues rocking with his hands over his ears. As he rocks, the paraprofessional gently kneads his arms. "These children often like tactile stimulation. I have one student who likes to have his head squeezed," says Gruber.

A Heterogeneous Disorder

There are other common traits that are helpful for general education teachers to understand, says Marguerite Colston of the Autism Society of America.

The social world is confusing to children with autism, and they don't pick up on cues that come naturally to others. They can't generalize, and don't realize that accepted behavior they've learned in one setting is appropriate for all settings: for example, table manners learned at home should also be practiced at school. They have selective attention and sometimes focus on one detail, such as the color of a car rather than the car itself. Later, they might not be able to identify another car if it's not the same color. They often engage in self-stimulatory activities, like rocking or hand flapping, to ease anxiety. Repetition and consistency are comforting—even slight changes to routines are distressing.

Still, autism is a heterogeneous disorder and, as Colston often says, "If you've met one child with autism, you've met one child with autism"—which is why effective interventions and therapies vary from child to child.

The research is consistent on this point: the earlier that special education staff begin helping children with autism

Defining the Terms *Mainstreaming* and *Inclusion*

There are many kinds of inclusion. In the past, the term *mainstreaming* was used to describe children who had been in special education and were being assisted to enter the "mainstream"—namely, regular education classes. The term *inclusion* is often now used preferentially or interchangeably with *mainstreaming*. Inclusion can be full (for the whole school day) or partial—meaning the child is assigned a special day class but also a general education class, where he typically spends more and more of his time as certain benchmarks are reached. There are also hybrid programs, especially in preschool programs, that are referred to as *integrated*, meaning some of the pupils have IEPs [individualized education programs] and some don't—because they are developing typically.

Bryna Siegel,
Getting the Best for Your Child with Autism, *2008.*

manage their differences, the better. In the Fair Lawn Public School District, children enter the autism program, called "Stepping Stones," at age three. Not all students from the program will be included in general education classes, but the goal is to prepare them for the possibility.

Domenica Bassora is a Stepping Stones teacher at Edison Preschool in Fair Lawn. She leads a team of paraprofessionals who work one-on-one with six preschoolers with autism. The curriculum in Bassora's classroom is based on Applied Behavioral Analysis (ABA), which provides a very structured interaction with the child, a defined set of goals, and a careful recording of progress.

At first, they work on basic attending skills, such as making eye contact and staying seated in a chair. Occupational therapists teach the students to walk up and down stairs or to roll a ball. Physical therapists help them with their motor skills, like holding a toothbrush or a crayon. Some children are even potty trained at school.

Speech-language pathologists work on improving communication skills, whether through a picture-symbol, sign language, or verbal system. If the student remains nonverbal, some learn to express themselves with assistive technology, which is expensive but can open up the world for a child with autism.

Paraprofessionals work on imitation skills, asking students to follow their lead as they clap their hands or put their hands on their head. The students are taught to wave or say hello and goodbye, to wait, to take turns, and to share.

In Bassora's classroom, the children sit in their own partitioned "cubbies," allowing them to feel cocooned and secure. On one wall of the cubbie is a pictorial schedule of activities so they always know what comes next, which eases transitions.

The Goal of Inclusion

When they graduate to the next step in the Stepping Stones program, the children work in twos in an open classroom environment where the beginning of each carefully scheduled activity is signaled by a bell. The students move from one work station to another where they develop more academic skills, always with the goal of inclusion.

"The general education teachers tell us what the students will need to do, and we work on those skills," says special education teacher Alison Pahlck. "We work on the components of letters by drawing lines and circles, and they learn to identify letters and numbers." In the fine motor skills center, they work to desensitize children to different substances like glue and finger paint. "This also helps build the muscle tone in their hands, which can be weak in children with autism," says Pahlck.

For some, like Nick, a ninth-grader at Central Kitsap Middle School in Kitsap, Washington, maintaining fine motor skills will be an ongoing struggle. Nick, 15, has a lot of trouble writing, and his hands begin to shake with fatigue after several minutes of typing on his Alpha Smart, a small, portable word processor.

Although he is able to spend most of the school day in general education classes, Nick also has ongoing academic challenges. Steve Coleman, a paraprofessional who works with middle school children with autism at Central Kitsap, says he finds ways to make academic work more palatable by engaging Nick in his particular areas of interest.

Like many of his classmates, Nick likes to watch the Discovery Channel and Animal Planet and is a big fan of video games. Unlike his classmates, he also likes to hide out in the library and is often overdressed in school, even on the hottest days, with his coat buttoned to the top and, until recently, a hood tied tightly over his head.

Nick and five other autistic students bookend their days in the special education classroom. In first period they work on social and behavioral skills; during last period, they debrief and work on study skills. They can also visit or stay in the special education classroom at any time during the day if they need a break.

An Opportunity to Teach Tolerance

As part of the inclusion process at Central Kitsap, students with autism can also serve as teaching assistants (TAs) for general education teachers. It's a volunteer position, performed after regular class work is completed. Nick is a TA for Julie Moore, of NEA's IDEA Resource Cadre, who is now a general education teacher at Nick's school.

He makes photocopies, three-hole punches papers, and completes clerical tasks. "I like the work. It makes me feel good," says Nick.

One of his proudest achievements was making a hallway bulletin board display of student work, including "Why High School Matters" bumper stickers created by his classmates. "Creativity doesn't come easily to Nick," says Moore. "This was a big deal for him."

So was being named Student of the Month in December. The best part, says Nick, was seeing his picture hang right alongside the other Students of the Month.

Most of the children in Nick's school treat him and the other autistic students with respect, or, at worst, with indifference, says Coleman. Just as they find Nick to be different, he finds them equally bewildering. Which is why Coleman says inclusion leads to one of education's most important lessons: "It's an opportunity to teach tolerance to all of the children."

> *"Different children may require different ways of learning and different amounts of assistance in school depending on how autistic they are."*

Mainstreaming May Not Benefit Autistic Students

Laura Madsen

In the following viewpoint, Laura Madsen asserts that the integration of autistic students into regular schools, which is called mainstreaming, can sometimes backfire. She explains that trained classroom staff should monitor autistic students to make sure they do not harm themselves or others. Such monitoring is not automatic and, where budgets are tight, often may not happen. Madsen cites examples where integration resulted in a negative school experience for autistic and nonautistic children. She concludes that mainstreaming may not work for some students who need extra attention. Laura Madsen writes the "Lady in Red," a blog covering a variety of subjects including food, fashion, entertainment, and mainstream topics in the media.

As you read, consider the following questions:

1. Why are schools taking a closer look at how to best educate autistic students and their classmates, according to the viewpoint?

2. What happened to the young son of Madsen's friend on the fourth day of school?

3. In the event described by the author, what happened to the child who drank the soapy paint solution?

I'm not an expert on autism, but from my understanding there is an autistic spectrum, where some children, may exhibit only some mild signs of autism—perhaps poor coordination, or they focus on certain things for longer periods of time than usual, or maybe they have tactile issues. Then, there are other children who display more severe autistic traits, and can have difficulty learning because of reduced attention spans, or maybe even display signs of aggression under circumstances where an observer can not understand why the child would act out in that manner. Different children may require different ways of learning and different amounts of assistance in school depending on how autistic they are.

Autism has always been around. However, either due to better diagnoses, or environmental influences, there are more cases of autism now than ever before. Because of this, schools are taking a closer look at students who are autistic and have tried to decide the best way to provide an education for them, as well as their classmates.

Until recently, I wasn't quite sure if all schools were like American schools when it came to how they place and assist autistic children in classrooms. In recent years, schools in the United States, and I've now also found out in England, as well, have started to mainstream autistic children into regular classrooms as much as possible. I think this is a good idea, for the most part. However, sometimes, this can backfire, big time.

A friend of mine, who lives in England, relayed to me a story about her five year-old son starting school. Like most children, he had the expectation that every other child is just like him. Why not? Most kids will smile at you, play with you, and are friendly right off the bat. However, it never occurred to this child's mother to tell her son that there may be children in his class that look just like him, and act just like him for the most part, but sometimes—they may need extra help, or they may not always act like he does.

Maybe sometimes they will get frustrated more easily, or they may cry and he may not understand why. And maybe, sometimes, there will be children that out-of-the-blue, although rare, may decide that they want to take out their frustration on him.

That's exactly what happened on his fourth day of school this year. Another little boy decided to pummel my friend's son to the ground in school. Thankfully, the boys were separated and no one was physically hurt. However, if you were a five year-old and had a classmate wallop you upside the head and knock you to the ground for no reason, with force, and intention, you would probably be pretty emotionally traumatized by it, and you definitely wouldn't understand why.

The boy that did the pouncing is autistic. I'm not saying that he is typical of all autistic children, but there are children, like him, who do need more attention than one teacher in the classroom, spreading her attention thin over 20–30 students, can give. (And yes, I also understand that a child who is not autistic can also act out and become violent as well. Of course this is not something isolated to autistic children.)

But while some people may think that I'm generalizing, I also question if it is right to broadly generalize that all autistic children should be "mainstreamed" into the classrooms where there is typically one teacher per 20 or more students. I don't think it's fair to the child that needs special help; and I don't think it's fair to the other students in the same class because those three or four children are taking time and attention away from them in school, causing distractions, and in this case, causing a problem. Not all autistic children that are placed in regular classrooms are given aides. It's not an automatic thing.

I know school budgets are tight. I know that many districts can not afford the cost of aides for many of these children. But what is the cost of NOT doing that? Will the children with autism that need additional supervision and instruction get less of an education as a result? What about the students that do not need extra help, but now have to share the same classrooms with children that monopolize the teacher's time with their behavioral issues? Are these students getting the time with the teacher that they need?

I'm not proposing across the board segregation. But I am proposing closer evaluation of some students who have special needs and consider placing them in classrooms where they can get the attention and support they need so they can safely and effectively learn in school, and others can, too.

I'll give you another example of mainstreaming gone wrong. Another woman I know was volunteering to help with a first grade activity. All of the first grade classes were participating, including, those children who were autistic. Some children had aides with them; some did not.

The woman was volunteering to lead a simple science experiment, consisting of setting up trays of water with a mild soap solution in them and some paint, so the children could make bubble paintings. She was told she needed to set up the trays and give activity instructions to the children in small groups. The groups changed tables and went from activity to activity.

She was never told that there were some special needs children in the groups that could require extra supervision. She knew that there were aides in the room, but thought that if a child was in the group without an aide, they did not re-

The Term *Mainstreaming* Is Doublespeak

Mainstreaming and *full inclusion* are positive words. They sound much better than saying that the school district can save money by partly or fully depriving a child of the special help he or she needs to best overcome a learning disability. The term *mainstreaming* is a great example of Orwellian doublespeak—implying that something that is nothing *is* something. If I sound negative about mainstreaming, I am. There is relatively little research on the effects of mainstreaming autistic children, and even less on full inclusion. What little research there is does not support the utility of mainstreaming for autistic and PDD [pervasive developmental disorder] children as it is most often carried out in public schools. Nevertheless, the PC (politically correct) revolution has launched mainstreaming as a keystone of special education policy in many areas in the United States.

Bryna Siegel, The World of the Autistic Child, *1996.*

quire any extra watching over. So this woman had the expectation that if she clearly explained to the six-year-olds to blow air through the straw to create bubbles, a few times, that the children, would do as they were told.

What happened was, the aides were busy taking pictures in the classroom and not watching the few children that really did need their help. The volunteer did not know by sight which children needed extra attention. One of the autistic children at the table wound up drinking some of the soapy paint solution as a result. The child was not hurt, but he had a bad taste in his mouth and blue teeth. (Understandably so.) After the parent volunteer realized what happened, she overheard one of the teachers call for the aide to come give the child some water so he could rinse out his mouth.

Should the aide be blamed? No one is perfect. Should the parent be blamed? No. She didn't know that the child generally did not follow instructions or needed special assistance. Should the parent have been made aware ahead of time that there were autistic children present and she should give certain ones extra attention—yes! Or, perhaps any children that were not able to participate at the expected level of a first grader in this experiment should have been given separate supervised instruction to begin with, for the safety and enjoyment of everyone.

My intention is not to say this because I want to make autistic children feel bad or different in a hurtful way. It's because, if I were the parent volunteer, I would not want anything to happen to any child. If you aren't aware of a special need, how can you address it?

Thankfully the soapy solution was not toxic and no one was worse for wear in the end. However, unless that school changes its policy of informing parents and volunteers about the potential situations they may get into as a result of unsupervised special needs children, I don't think she will be volunteering her time again—which is a shame.

Maybe some autistic children can assimilate into regular classroom environments without assistance; but maybe some can't. Maybe some need extra help. And maybe, mainstreaming isn't right for everyone all of the time.

> "The military's improper discharges will continue so long as there is pressure to reduce medical costs and so long as military recruitment standards remain artificially low due to strong public opposition to the current wars."

Veterans Should Not Be Wrongly Discharged for Personality Disorder

Paul Sullivan

In the following viewpoint, taken from congressional testimony, Paul Sullivan accuses the US Department of Defense (DoD) of improperly discharging veterans for personality disorder. First, the author points out that as many as twenty thousand veterans have been removed from service due to this and other unfounded diagnoses. Second, through this illegal practice, he argues, the DoD cuts costs on health care. and benefits, denying veterans and their families medical coverage, disability payments, and other benefits. Third, Sullivan contends that Congress should act to modernize military separation regulations, identify and amend previous improper discharges, and improve oversight and ac-

Paul Sullivan, "Statement of Paul Sullivan, Executive Director, Veterans for Common Sense," US House of Representatives Committee on Veterans' Affairs, Hearing on Personality Disorder Discharges: Impact on Veterans' Benefits, September 15, 2010.

countability of military health services. The author is executive director of the nonprofit Veterans for Common Sense (VCS) and served in the US Army during the Gulf War.

As you read, consider the following questions:

1. What evidence does Sullivan provide for suspicious diagnoses of personality disorder in the military?

2. As suggested by Sullivan, how much does the Department of Defense stand to gain from kicking out twenty thousand veterans from the military?

3. In the author's view, why is a proper diagnosis of personality disorder by psychiatrists imperative?

Veterans for Common Sense (VCS) thanks Committee Chairman [Bob] Filner, Ranking Member [Steve] Buyer, and Members of the Committee for inviting us to testify about the impact of improper Department of Defense (DoD) "personality disorder" discharges on our veterans seeking benefits from the Department of Veterans Affairs (VA).

VCS is here today because we remain alarmed that DoD continues improperly discharging our servicemembers who had entered the military in good health and served with honor while deployed to the Iraq and Afghanistan wars, only to be administratively discharged, often without access to medical care or benefits from DoD or VA.

We begin our testimony with an urgent request that Congress put an immediate stop to DoD's improper "personality disorder," "adjustment disorder," and "pattern of misconduct" discharges for servicemembers deployed to war since 2001.

The main underlying cause of the improper discharge remains the enormous pressure from top Pentagon officials, including Secretary [of Defense] Robert Gates himself, to curb military spending. A recent news article by [writer] Noel Brinkerhoff at www.AllGov.com is a recent example of significant pressure to reduce military medical spending: "With the Department of Defense staring at enormous cost increases for its health care program, Defense Secretary Robert Gates is proposing raising premiums for the first time ever since the creation of the TRICARE system [health care program of US military] in 1996."

VCS believes the military's improper discharges will continue so long as there is pressure to reduce medical costs and so long as military recruitment standards remain artificially low due to strong public opposition to the current wars.

Our testimony today focuses on three areas. First, how many of our Iraq and Afghanistan war veterans were improperly released by the military? Second, what are the financial incentives for our military to continue the policy, and what does it cost our veterans in terms of lost benefits? And, third, what are the solutions Congress can implement to repair the damage, and how do we prevent this from happening again?. . .

Thousands of Veterans Are Impacted

According to *Army Times* and U.S. Senator Christopher "Kit" Bond, discharges for "other designated physical or mental conditions not amounting to disability"—which includes adjustment disorder—have shot from 1,453 in 2006 to 3,844 in 2009.

The increase in personality disorder discharges skyrocketed 165 percent in 3 years without any plausible explanation from the military. Now, *Army Times* observed, "Over the same time, personality disorder discharges dropped from a peak of 1,072 in 2006 to just 260 last year." In 2007, one estimate of the total number of improper discharges was as high as 20,000 based on an investigation by *The Nation* magazine.

Congress and advocates need additional accurate and consistent information in order to understand the full scope of this issue. VCS urges Congress to demand that the military produce statistics on the number of "personality disorder," "adjustment disorder," and "pattern of misconduct" discharges, every year since 2001, sorted by deployment status and military branch. DoD's refusal to release all of the data to Senators speaks volumes about DoD's intent to conceal this problem from Congress, continue the improper discharges, and otherwise avoid a proper resolution.

Based on the limited statistics available, VCS believes the military switched from "personality disorder" discharges to "adjustment disorder discharges" after this Committee exposed "personality disorder" discharges during a July 2007 hearing.

Again, quoting *Army Times*, "Jason Perry, a former Army judge advocate who helps troops going through medical retirement, said he has seen dozens of such cases. 'It's very common. And it's completely illegal.'" In our view, the military was caught by investigative reporter Joshua Kors at *The Nation* magazine. In response to his investigation, and subsequent Congressional hearings featuring veterans and advocates, the military did change the rules. Shortly thereafter, the military went back to the department's old ways, simply changing a few words on servicemembers' discharge forms and continuing the same shameful, outrageous, and improper practice.

From our 2007 testimony, VCS restates the obvious. Using the "personality disorder," "adjustment disorder," or "pattern of misconduct" discharges to remove servicemembers who served honorably during war is wrong and a violation of military regulations. Our servicemembers need medical exams and medical care, not improper discharges creating a cloud over their military service and access to VA care....

Who Wins and Who Loses?

Who wins and who loses? The answer is obvious. The military wins while our veterans and local governments lose. The military's illegal activity means DoD spends less on health care and benefits during a time of tight budgets. Our veterans and families lose because some won't receive urgently needed health care, disability payments, and other VA benefits. When VA does not provide care, then state and local governments pick up the tab.

The losses to our veterans are staggering. The average cost for VA care and benefits, over a period of 40 years, is between $500,000 to $1,000,000 per veteran. To date, DoD stands to illegally deny between $5 billion to $20 billion in lifetime health care and benefits to the estimated 10,000 to 20,000 veterans improperly kicked out by the military. This estimate is based on the academic research found in the book, *The Three Trillion Dollar War*, by Linda Bilmes and Joseph Stiglitz, published in 2008. The authors estimate that the lifetime medical and benefit costs for our deployed Iraq and Afghanistan war veterans may be $500 billion or higher for nearly one million patients and claims.

Based on our conversations with veterans, those with "personality disorder" discharges frequently believe they are not entitled to full VA benefits. In many cases, that's partly true. VA is supposed to provide 5 years of free medical care for veterans who deployed to a war zone after November 11, 1998 (except those with a dishonorable discharge). There are plenty of examples of veterans diagnosed with post-traumatic stress disorder (PTSD) and/or traumatic brain injury (TBI) who urgently need VA care and benefits for those conditions. However, they either do not seek VA care, they are unreasonably delayed in obtaining care due to VA paperwork nightmares, or they are denied care by VA.

Some non-medical VA benefits may be lost by veterans with improper "personality disorder" discharges. For example, an early release from active duty may block access to VA's home loan guaranty and education benefits.

PTSD symptoms may mimic "personality disorder" discharges with anger, self-medicating, and minor infractions. A proper diagnosis by a psychologist or psychiatrist is imperative, rather than DoD's current process of rushing veterans through a non-medical administrative discharge. According to DoD and VA policy, if PTSD symptoms last longer than 6 months, then the veteran's diagnosis should be changed to PTSD. With a PTSD diagnosis, a veteran may be medically retired with an honorable discharge, a disability rating of at least 50 percent, and free medical care.

In the worst case examples of lost benefits among veterans, VA has improperly denied veterans' PTSD disability compensation claim because the veterans' DD-214 [discharge form] listed "personality disorder," even when the veterans had deployed to a war zone, were diagnosed with PTSD, and were clearly given an improper military discharge. . . .

What Are the Solutions?

VCS urges Congress to take several steps toward resolving the crisis of improper military discharges often preventing access to VA services for our Iraq and Afghanistan war veterans. These steps include modernizing military separation regulations, identifying and righting past inappropriate discharges, and dramatically improving oversight and accountability of military health surveillance. VCS encourages veterans to seek care and benefits at VA, without fear of discrimination or stigma. An improper discharge by the military may unfairly stigmatize a veteran and impede access to health care, benefits, and employment that are often vital for a smooth transition from combat to community.

| "*The Army is dedicated to making sure that all Soldiers with physical and mental conditions caused by wartime service receive the care they deserve.*"

Discharged Veterans Are Thoroughly Evaluated for Personality Disorder

Gina S. Farrisee

Gina S. Farrisee is director of the US Army's Department of Military Personnel Management. In the following viewpoint, Farrisee insists that veterans who are discharged due to personality disorder first undergo documented and careful evaluations. Due to the concern that they instead suffer from post-traumatic stress disorder (PTSD) or traumatic brain injury (TBI), the army's Office of the Surgeon General has mandated screening for PTSD and TBI in such discharges along with enhanced requirements, Farrisee maintains. Also, commanders maximize the use of counseling and rehabilitation, the author asserts, before it is determined that a veteran can no longer serve the military. Finally, Farrisee explains that those discharged are offered additional counseling and assistance regarding employment, education, health, and other areas.

Gina S. Farrisee, "Statement of Major General Gina S. Farrisee, Director, Department of Military Personnel Management, G-1, Department of the Army, US Department of Defense," US House of Representatives Committee on Veterans' Affairs, Hearing on Personality Disorder Discharges: Impact on Veterans' Benefits, September 15, 2010.

order, that a personality disorder diagnosis be corroborated by a peer or higher-level mental health professional (Medical Treatment Facility Chief of Behavioral Health or equivalent official), that the personality disorder diagnosis be endorsed by the Director, Proponency of Behavioral Health, Office of the Surgeon General, and that the diagnosis address PTSD or other co-morbid mental illness, if present. The Army also provided for the distinction between Soldiers who were separated for personality disorder who had less than 2 years time in service with Soldiers with 2 or more years of service.

A Maximum Use of Counseling and Rehabilitation

Commanders make maximum use of counseling and rehabilitation before determining that a Soldier has limited potential for further military service and, therefore, should be separated. When a Soldier's conduct or performance becomes unacceptable, the commander will ensure that the Soldier is formally counseled on his or her deficiencies and given a reasonable opportunity to overcome or correct them. If the commander believes a medical issue may be the basis of the misconduct or poor performance, the commander refers the Soldier for a medical evaluation. Separation for personality disorder is authorized only if the diagnosis concludes that the disorder is so severe that the Soldier's ability to function effectively in the military environment is significantly impaired. The Soldier is counseled that the diagnosis of a personality disorder does not qualify as a disability. When it is determined that separation for personality disorder is appropriate, the unit commander takes action to notify the Soldier. Separation authority for personality disorder for Soldiers who are or have been deployed to an area designated as an imminent-danger pay area is the General Court Martial Convening Authority (General Officer–level commander). In all other cases, the separation authority is the Special Court Martial Convening Authority (Colonel-level commander).

Separated Soldiers may request review and change of their discharge by petitioning the Army Review Boards Agency (ARBA). ARBA's case management division screening team hand carries these cases to the Army Discharge Review Board (ADRB), which prioritizes review and boarding of applications for upgrades or changes in discharges where either PTSD or TBI is diagnosed. ARBA's Medical Advisor serves as a voting board member when PTSD/TBI cases are boarded by the ADRB.

The Army Career and Alumni Program

Soldiers who are separated from Active Duty prior to their actual separation date, also known as unanticipated losses, are fully eligible for all transition services provided by the Army Career and Alumni Program (ACAP). Programs available for Soldiers within ACAP include pre-separation counseling, employment assistance, Veterans Benefits Briefing, and the Disabled Transition Assistance Program (DTAP).

Pre-separation counseling provides Soldiers information about services and benefits they have earned while on active duty. The following areas are covered in this counseling: effects of a career change, employment assistance, relocation assistance, education and training, health and life insurance, finances, Reserve affiliation, Veterans benefits, Disabled Veterans benefits, post government service employment restriction and an Individual Transition Plan. Each of these areas have several items that support the specific area. This pre-separation counseling is mandatory for all separating Soldiers who have at least 180 days of active duty upon time of separation.

Employment assistance consists of individual one-on-one counseling, attending a Department of Labor two-and-a-half days long employment workshop, finalizing a resume, practice employment interviews, using various automated employment tools and using the Internet to access job data banks. This is strictly voluntary; Soldiers do not have to participate.

The Veterans Benefits Briefing is a 4-hour long briefing provided by Veterans Affairs (VA) counselors covering all VA-controlled services and benefits that a Soldier can receive or may be eligible for after separation. Transition counselors strongly encourage separating Soldiers to attend.

The Disabled Transition Assistance Program (DTAP) is a 2-hour long briefing provided by VA counselors. Soldiers who are separated due to medical or physical injuries, as well as Soldiers who believe that they will file a VA Disability Claim, are highly encouraged to attend this briefing.

Soldiers out-processing as an unanticipated loss normally have limited time remaining on active duty and will in almost all cases have insufficient time to take advantage of the above programs except for the legally-mandated pre-separation counseling. However, these Soldiers are fully eligible to receive these services for up to 180 days after separation. Additionally, they are referred by the transition counselor to go to the nearest Department of Labor Career One Stop after separation for assistance in obtaining employment and are instructed to use the VA E-benefits Web site to obtain information concerning their eligibility for VA benefits.

Maintaining Oversight on PTSD and TBI

The Army remains dedicated to making sure that all Soldiers with physical and mental conditions caused by wartime service receive the care they deserve. The Army is grateful for the continued support of Congress for providing for the well-being of the best Army in the world.

The Army leadership has confidence in our behavioral health providers and the policies in place to ensure proper treatment for our Soldiers. We continue to monitor these processes to ensure the accurate diagnosis of PTSD and TBI and to further corroborate each diagnosis of personality disorder.

Veterans who feel that they were discharged inappropriately are encouraged to seek a remedy through the Army Review Boards Agency (ARBA).

The mental and physical well-being of our Soldiers and Veterans depends on your tremendous support. We must continue to maintain an appropriate level of oversight on PTSD and TBI, wounds all too frequently associated with the signature weapon of this war, the improvised explosive device. The men and women of our Army deserve this; we owe this to them. The Army is committed to continuing to improve the accuracy and efficiency of these policies and their implementation. Thank you for the opportunity to appear before you this morning. I look forward to answering any questions you may have.

Periodical and Internet Sources Bibliography

The following articles have been selected to supplement the diverse views presented in this chapter.

Allan G. Breed	"In Tide of PTSD Cases, Fear of Fraud Growing," *Army Times*, May 2, 2010.
James Dao	"Branding a Soldier with 'Personality Disorder,'" *New York Times*, February 24, 2012.
Allen Frances	"DSM5 Temper Dysregulation—Good Intentions, Bad Solution," DSM5 in Distress Blog, *Psychology Today*, April 8, 2010. www.psychologytoday.com.
Craig Goodall	"My Autistic Child," *SEN Magazine*, August 22, 2012.
Joshua Kors	"Disposable Soldiers," *The Nation*, April 26, 2010.
Dorothy Lepkowska	"Why Don't You Understand? The Difficulties of Teaching Autistic Children," *The Guardian* (UK), November 10, 2008.
Maia Szalavitz	"Why Autistic Kids Make Easy Targets for School Bullies," *Time*, September 5, 2012.
U.S. Medicine	"Legislators, Military, and Veterans Advocates Clash over Discharges," October 2010.
Shirley S. Wang	"The Long Battle to Rethink Mental Illness in Children," *Wall Street Journal*, October 18, 2012.
Patricia Wen	"Proposed Diagnosis for Bipolar Disorder Divides Psychiatrists," *Boston Globe*, May 10, 2012.

For Further Discussion

Chapter 1

1. Zinnia Jones contends that claims disputing the validity or prevalence of attention-deficit/hyperactivity disorder (ADHD) in children are conspiracy theories. In your view, is Fred Baughman's position that ADHD is promoted for profit by the psychiatry and pharmaceutical industries such a theory? Why or why not?

2. Jon Ronson maintains that the diagnosis of childhood bipolar disorder is based on "superficial behaviors" that include normal tendencies in children. In your opinion, does Ronson make a persuasive argument? Why or why not? Use examples from the text to support your answer.

Chapter 2

1. According to Anita Thapar, as quoted by Penny Bailey, research has identified the genetic variant for ADHD and established that the disorder is hereditary. Peter Gray, however, also points to increased competitiveness in education and new diagnostic measures causing a rise in ADHD. In your view, which author offers the more convincing explanation? Cite examples from the viewpoints to explain your answer.

2. Michael Snyder warns that thimerosal, a vaccine preservative that contains mercury, is directly linked to autism and its epidemic rate in the United States. On the contrary, Sharon Begley insists that a major study claiming to establish this link is flawed. In your opinion, does the evidence that Begley provides debunk Snyder's argument? Why or why not?

3. Sally Satel suggests that the difficulties in readjusting to normal life among war veterans is frequently mislabeled as

post-traumatic stress disorder (PTSD). Do you agree or disagree with the author? Use examples from the text to support your response.

Chapter 3

1. Caroline Miller declares that even when they no longer are effective, stimulant medications for children with ADHD are beneficial. Nonetheless, Edmund S. Higgins claims that the medications have possible long-term side effects. In your view, do the potential benefits of ADHD medications outweigh the potential side effects? Cite examples from the viewpoints to explain your answer.

2. A supporter of medical marijuana, Steve Fox acknowledges that evidence for its treatment of PTSD is limited and anecdotal. In your opinion, does this strengthen opponents' assertions against medical marijuana as a medication option? Why or why not?

Chapter 4

1. Laura Madsen argues that mainstreaming may not be appropriate for all autistic children and may even harm them or their classmates. In your view, does Cindy Long, who supports mainstreaming autistic students, provide observations that disprove Madsen's arguments? Why or why not?

2. Gina S. Farrisee explains that the concern that veterans with PTSD or brain injuries have been wrongly discharged for having personality disorders resulted in mandatory screening and enhanced requirements in these evaluations. In your opinion, do the changes she describes satisfactorily address Paul Sullivan's concerns? Cite examples from the viewpoints to explain your answer.

Organizations to Contact

The editors have compiled the following list of organizations concerned with the issues debated in this book. The descriptions are derived from materials provided by the organizations. All have publications or information available for interested readers. The list was compiled on the date of publication of the present volume; the information provided here may change. Be aware that many organizations take several weeks or longer to respond to inquiries, so allow as much time as possible.

American Academy of Child and Adolescent
Psychiatry (AACAP)
3615 Wisconsin Ave. NW, Washington, DC   20016-3007
(202) 966-7300 • fax: (202) 966-2891
e-mail: communications@aacap.org
website: www.aacap.org

AACAP is a nonprofit professional organization that supports and advances child and adolescent psychiatry through research and education. The academy's goal is to provide information that will remove the stigma associated with mental illnesses and ensure proper treatment for children who suffer from mental or behavioral disorders. It publishes the monthly *Journal of the American Academy of Child and Adolescent Psychiatry* and the series Facts for Families in several languages.

American Academy of Pediatrics (AAP)
141 Northwest Point Blvd., Elk Grove Village, IL   60007-1098
(847) 434-4000 • fax: (847) 434-8000
website: www.aap.org

AAP is a professional member organization of pediatricians in the United States, Canada, and Latin America who work together to address the health needs of children. The academy publishes several periodicals, including the monthly journal *Pediatrics* and monthly newsletter *AAP News*. Its website includes a Parent Resources section as well as an online bookstore.

American Psychological Association (APA)
750 First Street NE, Washington, DC   20002-4242
(202) 336-5500; toll-free: (800) 374-2721
e-mail: public.affairs@apa.org
website: www.apa.org

The APA is the largest scientific and professional organization representing psychology in the United States and the world's largest association of psychologists. Its mission is to advance the creation, communication, and application of psychological knowledge to benefit society and improve people's lives. The association publishes books and guides for professionals and the public, the magazine *Monitor on Psychology*, and several newsletters. Its website offers information on attention-deficit/hyperactivity disorder, autism, obsessive-compulsive disorder, post-traumatic stress disorder, and other behavioral disorders.

Anxiety and Depression Association of America (ADAA)
8701 Georgia Ave., Suite 412, Silver Spring, MD   20910
(240) 385-1001 • fax: (240) 485-1035
website: www.adaa.org

ADAA is a national nonprofit organization dedicated to the prevention, treatment, and cure of anxiety, depression, and related disorders and to improving the lives of all people who suffer from them. It disseminates information, provides links to those who need treatment, and advocates cost-effective treatments. On its website, ADAA offers educational brochures on various disorders and the quarterly e-newsletter *Triumph*.

Attention Deficit Disorder Association (ADDA)
PO Box 7557, Wilmington, DE   19803-9997
phone/fax: (800) 939-1019
e-mail: info@add.org
website: www.add.org

ADDA is a national nonprofit organization whose mission is to provide information, resources, and networking opportunities to help adults with ADHD lead better lives. It provides fact sheets and articles on ADHD, a section on awareness and advocacy, and an online bookstore on its website.

Autism Research Institute (ARI)

4182 Adams Ave., San Diego, CA   92116
(866) 366-3361
website: www.autism.com

Established in 1967 by psychologist and renowned father of modern autism research Dr. Bernard Rimland, ARI continues research, outreach, and cooperative efforts with other organizations worldwide. It advocates for the rights of people with autism spectrum disorder and operates without funding from special-interest groups. The organization publishes several electronic newsletters, and its website offers fact sheets and links to other autism organizations.

Autism Society

4340 East-West Highway, Suite 350, Bethesda, MD   20814
(301) 657-0881; toll-free: (800) 328-8476 • fax: (301) 657-0869
e-mail: info@autism-society.org
website: www.autism-society.org

The Autism Society is one of the largest grassroots autism support and advocacy groups in the United States. It provides information and referrals to autism services nationwide, with a mission to increase public awareness of autism and help individuals with autism and their families deal with day-to-day issues. The ASA publishes the *Autism Advocate*.

Autism Speaks

1 E. Thirty-Third Street, 4th Floor, New York, NY   10016
(212) 252-8584 • fax: (212) 252-8676
e-mail: research@autismspeaks.org
website: www.autismspeaks.org

Autism Speaks was founded in February 2005 by Bob and Suzanne Wright, grandparents of a child with autism. This national organization promotes public awareness of autism and works to fund research into the causes, prevention, and treatment of autism. It distributes the *e-Speaks* newsletter and offers a resource guide, autism apps, and tool kits on its website.

Children and Adults with
Attention-Deficit/Hyperactivity Disorder (CHADD)
8181 Professional Place, Suite 150, Landover, MD   20785
(301) 306-7070; toll-free: (800) 233-4050 • fax: (301) 306-7090
website: www.chadd.org

CHADD is a nonprofit organization founded by a group of concerned parents that works to improve the lives of children and adults with ADHD through education, advocacy, and support. It publishes the bimonthly *Attention!* magazine, books, and many fact sheets about the disorder.

Institute for Vaccine Safety (IVS)
Johns Hopkins University Bloomberg School of Public Health
Baltimore, MD   21205
e-mail: info@hopkinsvaccine.org
website: www.vaccinesafety.edu

The institute's mission is to provide an independent assessment of vaccines and vaccine safety to help guide decision makers and educate physicians, the public, and the media about key issues surrounding the safety of vaccines. It aims to prevent disease by promoting usage of the safest vaccines possible. Information concerning the autism/vaccine link is available on its website.

International OCD Foundation (IOCDF)
PO Box 961029, Boston, MA   02196
(617) 973-5801
website: www.ocdfoundation.org

IOCDF is a multinational organization that serves those who are affected by obsessive-compulsive disorder (OCD) and other related neurobiological spectrum disorders. The mission and goals of the foundation are to educate the public and professionals about OCD in order to raise awareness and improve the quality of treatment provided; support research into the cause of, and effective treatments for, OCD and related disorders; improve access to resources for those with OCD and their families; and advocate and lobby for the OCD community. IOCDF offers brochures, fact sheets, books, and multimedia online.

National Alliance on Mental Illness (NAMI)
3803 N. Fairfax Drive, Suite 100, Arlington, VA   22203
(703) 524-7600 • fax: (703) 524-9094
website: www.nami.org

NAMI is a national grassroots mental health organization dedicated to building better lives for the millions of Americans affected by mental illness. The organization publishes a magazine called the *Advocate* and provides information about specific mental illnesses, treatment, support, and programs on its website.

National Autism Association (NAA)
20 Alice Agnew Drive, Attleboro Falls, MA   02763
(877) 622-2884 • fax: (774) 643-6331
website: http://nationalautismassociation.org

NAA is a parent-led nonprofit organization that focuses on autism research, advocacy, education, and support for those affected by autism. Its website publishes research findings, brochures, and press releases.

National Center for PTSD
US Department of Veterans Affairs, Washington, DC   20420
(802) 296-6300
e-mail: nptsd@va.gov
website: www.ptsd.va.gov

Part of the Department of Veterans Affairs (VA), the center conducts research and promotes education on the prevention, understanding, and treatment of post-traumatic stress disorder (PTSD). Although it is a VA center, its seven divisions across the country provide expertise on all types of trauma—from natural disasters, terrorism, violence, and abuse to combat exposure. On its website, the center offers overviews on PTSD, its assessment, and its treatment; information specific to women; mobile apps; videos; and web links.

National Institute of Mental Health (NIMH)
Science Writing, Press, and Dissemination Branch
Bethesda, MD   20892-9663
(301) 443-4513 • fax: (301) 443-4279
e-mail: nimhinfo@nih.gov
website: www.nimh.nih.gov

NIMH is the federal agency concerned with mental health research. It plans and conducts a comprehensive program of research relating to the causes, prevention, diagnosis, and treatment of mental illnesses. NIMH produces various informational publications on mental disorders and their treatment, including the booklets *Attention Deficit Hyperactivity Disorder, Bipolar Disorder in Children and Adolescents, Depression and College Students,* and *Anxiety Disorders.*

National Vaccine Information Center (NVIC)
407 Church Street, Suite H, Vienna, VA   22180
(703) 938-0342 • fax: (703) 938-5768
e-mail: contactnvic@gmail.com
website: www.nvic.org

Founded by parents of children injured by vaccines, NVIC is responsible for launching the vaccine safety and informed-consent movement in America in the early 1980s. The center is the oldest and largest consumer organization advocating the institution of vaccine safety and informed-consent protections in the mass vaccination system. On its website, NVIC publishes FAQs on vaccine laws and a free newsletter.

Bibliography of Books

Lee Baer   *The Imp of the Mind: Exploring the Silent Epidemic of Obsessive Bad Thoughts*. New York: Dutton, 2001.

Rita Nakashima Brock and Gabriella Lettini   *Soul Repair: Recovering from Moral Injury After War*. Boston: Beacon, 2012.

Terri Cheney   *The Dark Side of Innocence: Growing Up Bipolar*. New York: Atria Books, 2011.

Lawrence H. Diller   *Remembering Ritalin: A Doctor and Generation Rx Reflect on Life and Psychiatric Drugs*. New York: Penguin, 2011.

Erin P. Finley   *Fields of Combat: Understanding PTSD Among Veterans of Iraq and Afghanistan*. Ithaca, NY: ILR Press, 2011.

Arthur Fleischmann with Carly Fleischmann   *Carly's Voice: Breaking Through Autism*. New York: Simon & Schuster, 2012.

Michael J. Goldberg with Elyse Goldberg   *The Myth of Autism: How a Misunderstood Epidemic Is Destroying Our Children*. New York: Skyhorse, 2011.

Temple Grandin and Richard Panek   *The Autistic Brain: Thinking Across the Spectrum*. Boston: Houghton Mifflin Harcourt, 2013.

Ross W. Greene — *The Explosive Child: A New Approach for Understanding and Parenting Easily Frustrated, Chronically Inflexible Children*. New York: HarperCollins, 2010.

Edward M. Hallowell and John J. Ratey — *Driven to Distraction: Recognizing and Coping with Attention Deficit Disorder from Childhood Through Adulthood*. New York: Anchor Books, 2011.

Marla Handy — *No Comfort Zone: Notes on Living with Post Traumatic Stress Disorder*. Madison, WI: Mocassa, 2010.

Charles W. Hoge — *Once a Warrior, Always a Warrior: Navigating the Transition from Combat to Home—Including Combat Stress, PTSD, and mTBI*. Guilford, CT: GPP Life, 2010.

Stuart L. Kaplan — *Your Child Does Not Have Bipolar Disorder: How Bad Science and Good Public Relations Created the Diagnosis*. Santa Barbara, CA: Praeger, 2011.

Beth Alison Maloney — *Saving Sammy: Curing the Boy Who Caught OCD*. New York: Crown, 2009.

Kate McLaughlin — *Mommy, I'm Still in Here: Raising Children with Bipolar Disorder*. Lake Forest, CA: Behler, 2007.

Robert Melillo	*Autism: The Scientific Truth About Preventing, Diagnosing, and Treating Autism Spectrum Disorders—and What Parents Can Do Now.* New York: Penguin, 2013.
Seth Mnookin	*The Panic Virus: A True Story of Medicine, Science, and Fear.* New York: Simon & Schuster, 2011.
Paul A. Offit	*Autism's False Prophets: Bad Science, Risky Medicine, and the Search for a Cure.* New York: Columbia University Press, 2008.
Sharna Olfman, ed.	*Bipolar Children: Cutting-Edge Controversy, Insights, and Research.* Westport, CT: Praeger, 2007.
Dan Olmsted and Mark Blaxill	*The Age of Autism: Mercury, Medicine, and a Man-Made Epidemic.* New York: Thomas Dunne Books/St. Martin's, 2010.
Christal Presley	*Thirty Days with My Father: Finding Peace from Wartime PTSD.* Deerfield Beach, FL: Health Communications, 2012.
John Elder Robison	*Look Me in the Eye: My Life with Asperger's.* New York: Crown, 2007.
Elizabeth E. Root	*Kids Caught in the Psychiatric Maelstrom: How Pathological Labels and "Therapeutic" Drugs Hurt Children and Families.* Santa Barbara, CA: Praeger, 2009.

Andrew J.
Wakefield

Callous Disregard: Autism and Vaccines—the Truth Behind a Tragedy. New York: Skyhorse, 2010.

Leeann Whiffen

A Child's Journey Out of Autism: One Family's Story of Living in Hope and Finding a Cure. Naperville, IL: Sourcebooks, 2009.

Fletcher
Wortmann

Triggered: A Memoir of Obsessive-Compulsive Disorder. New York: Thomas Dunne Books/St. Martin's, 2012.

Index

A

O

Obama, Barack, 99

Obsessive-compulsive disorder
  (OCD)
   causation theories, 53–54
   cognitive behavioral interventions, 166–167
   description, 164
   ERP treatment, 163–168
   Intensive Outpatient Programs, 168
   metaphor use, for understanding, 165–167
   pharmacologic treatment, 167, 168
   storytelling treatment component, 165
   therapist choice, 167–168

OC (obsessive-compulsive) Foundation, 168

Offit, Paul, 83, 87, 89

Oklahoma City bombing, 103

O'Leary, John, 81, 83

Omnibus Autism Proceeding, 171, 172

Operation Enduring Freedom, 101

Operation Iraqi Freedom, 101

Oppositional defiant disorder
  (ODD), 41

The Oprah Winfrey Show (TV
  program), 87

The Other Side of ADHD
  (Southall), 65

P

Pahlck, Alison, 179–180

Panic disorder, 46

Parenting the Strong-Willed Child
  (Forehand and Long), 145

Parents
   ADHD and genetics, 55–60
   ADHD children, 25, 34, 60, 149
   bipolar disorder children, 38, 44, 47, 50
   books on ADHD parenting, 145–146
   skills training benefits, 144–145
   vaccination decisions, 70–73, 75–76

Parkinson's disease, 141–142

Pavuluri, Mani, 35–42

Pear, Tom, 106

Pelham, William, 145, 146

Personality disorder. *See* Veterans
  with personality disorder

Pervasive development disorder
  (PDD), 186

Peters, Joey, 156–162

PLAY Study Findings (Project to
  Learn about ADHD in Youth),
  127

Poling, Hannah, 90

The Politics of Readjustment: Vietnam Veterans Since the War
  (Scott), 108

Post-Traumatic Stress Disorder
  (PTSD)
   APA official recognition, 107–109
   developmental circumstances, 103–104
   DSM symptoms, 102–103, 108–109
   Journal of Traumatic Stress
  articles, 94, 103
   medical marijuana potential, 156–162
   rape victims, 103, 109

Veterans with traumatic brain injury (TBI), 92, 192, 195
  Army Review Boards Agency decisions, 198
  Army treatment dedication, 195
  oversight maintenance, 199–200
  pre-/post-separation services, 198–199
  separation policies, 196–197
Vietnam War era, 101, 106–107, 113–115
Violence, soldiers with PTSD, 94–95
Virtual reality exposure therapy (VRET), 121–122
Virtual Vietnam (computer technology), 121
Vitiello, Benedetto, 149
Vyvanse (amphetamine), 134

W

Wakefield, Andrew, 79–80, 82–85, 88, 90

Walter Reed Army Institute of Research, 104
Wang, Gene-Jack, 130
Webster-Stratton, Carolyn, 145–146
Weg, Allen, 163–168
Weldon, Dave, 86
Wellcome Trust gene study, 57–58
West Haven Veterans Affairs Medical Center (CT), 113–114
Williams, Josh, 96, 99
Wing, Lorna, 14
Winston, Andrew, 96
The World of the Autistic Child (Siegel), 186
World War I, 96
World War II, 96, 107, 116

Y

Yacovelli, Kathleen, 95
Yale University School of Medicine, 140
Young, Susan, 26
Your Defiant Child (Barkley), 146

CPSIA information can be obtained
at www.ICGtesting.com
Printed in the USA
FFOW01n1620060214